AMEN, AMEN, AMEN

Life's Journey
and Peaceful Minds
Through Chaotic Battles

By Donna Defelice

A wholly owned subsidary of **TBN**

DEDICATION

I want to dedicate this book to my lovely children: Nicholas, Christopher, and my daughter, Krystal. *God* has a plan and a purpose for my life and yours. Ask Him to show you His purpose for your life, and when He knows you are fully committed to it, then it will be revealed. When you have an encounter with *God*, listen to His voice and carry out His instructions for your life. This will allow for His will to be done on earth as it is in heaven.

I would also like to dedicate this book to my family, friends, and my co-workers. I spent much of my time with them talking about writing this book. People will come in and out of your life to fulfill the plan that He has for your life and in theirs for that period of time. So much will get accomplished for His kingdom, and everything will be fulfilled according to the purpose He has for you. *God* loves you so much He gave us *Jesus*, His only begotten Son, to die for us. Now we can have His comfort, known as the *Holy Spirit*, to guide us through our lives. This is heaven on earth, giving us peace of mind. While we are going through our trials here on earth, we are also at the same time with *God* in heaven. Whenever you have Jesus, you have everything, even when you have nothing. Spread the word of *God* throughout your life in order to touch the heart of other people. While you wait for the return of our Lord and Savior, praise *God* and all His glory!

Dear Heavenly Father, I want everything You have planned for me and my family's life to be accomplished, fulfilled, and completed forever and ever, in Jesus' name, Amen, Amen, and Amen!

ACKNOWLEDGMENTS

Ten years ago, I started to write this book after reading *Lioness Arising: Wake Up and Change Your World.* This book motivated me to start to write my book; it is a wonderful book. After many years later, a friend of mine gifted me the book *Idea to Print.* After reading it, I was motivated to write again, only this time to finish writing my book. This is an excellent read.

TABLE OF CONTENTS

INTRODUCTION

I just finished a ladies' bible Bible study at my church. We have been studying *Lioness Arising: Wake Up and Change Your World* by Lisa Bevere. Her book inspired me greatly to take action in my life. She writes about being a lioness, wakening up, being fierce, bold, having a voice, and changing your world by you making a change. I encourage anyone and everyone to read her book if they have a chance. This book has become a great blessing to my life because it helped me decided to write my own book. As you are reading about my journey and the way my life unfolded over the years, I want you to correlate your personal life events in order to establish a connection to *God*, sparking the fire inside of you. I want my trials and tribulations to be a blessing in your life. *God* is alive, and *Jesus* is the way! In this book, I want to share my supernatural encounter with *God* and *Jesus* from when I was fourteen years old. This experience was beyond anything you can imagine, and it changed my reality with just one breath. Before you read this book, take your mind out of the natural way of thinking, which is bond by time, space, matter, energy, and motion. Now, think like *God*, who is boundless, timeless, everywhere, everything, the light, and the power behind this book. Before I get into this majestic encounter, I first would like to share with you my life events leading up to this very special day that I had. As you are reading this book, I would like you to realize that I only remembered this a very short time after I woke up. I was later gracefully allowed to remember this experience with *God* that I now get to share with you.

EARLY LIFE
(FIVE TO FOURTEEN YEARS OF AGE)

"Donna, most kids your age are out playing; why are you sitting here talking with an old lady like me?" This quote is from my oldest friend and neighbor Irene, who I called Bun. This is what started my thinking about my life of what was important to me. Bun was very influential to me at a young age. Bun and I spent many hours talking on her front porch, spending quality time together. This one day, I drove her up to her old campground site. On the way there, we stopped at a small grocery store, purchased lunch meat for sandwiches, cold pasta, chips, and drinks. We had ourselves a picnic along with her memories from her past. She was so appreciative that I took the time to spend the whole day with her. Bun and I have connected in this special way that whenever I was getting married for the first time, I had asked her to be my grandmother at my wedding. She was so honored that I asked her. Then she replied, "My own grandchildren didn't even acknowledge me as their grandmother in their wedding." She told me that she felt deserted from her own family. I replied, "I would be honored for you to be my grandmother at my wedding." All my grandparents died before I was ten years old. I didn't have the experience of having grandparents in my life while I was growing up. I didn't realize how much this quote meant to me throughout my whole life until most recently; this is why I want to take the time to mention the people in my life who were special to me in building my relationships.

Now I am taking time here remembering the people who God has put in my life over the course of my life who have inspired me. Starting when I was five years old, my preacher at the Church of Christ in Connellsville, Pennsylvania, was preaching, walking back and forth on the platform, taking a white handkerchief, wiping the sweat dripping off his fore- head. I know the church did not have air conditioning back then, just big white ceiling fans that went around in circles, mostly at a slow speed. I was laying down on the church pew, wondering what D. S. was preaching about to have him preaching his heart out. I could not understand it. Then I was saying to myself, "I wish I knew what he was preaching about." Then immediately, I could hear and understand what he was preaching about. It has been so long ago; I believe he was saying that we were Christian soldiers marching on and something about little ants, putting the armor of God on for protection. I just know he has inspired me by the effort he put into his preaching. I knew it was very important.

I remember staying overnight at my cousin's house as I was growing up. My Uncle Gene and Aunt Sandy would take me to church with them. We would always be late for church, and my cousin would comment. I would be surprised if we made it to church at all, but we would always make it to church. Usually, it was really late. I always enjoyed going to church with them. My family did not go at this point in my life; sometimes, they would go to church for a period of time, then stop going altogether. I don't know to this day why they would ever quit going to church. Well, my cousin Sharon was reading her Bible, and I started to ask her questions about it. Then my cousin and I would take turns reading the Bible; she encouraged me to read my Bible, showed me how important it was to read your Bible. She was smart and knew a lot about the Bible. I remember R. W., my preacher's son, and Sharon would have flashcards about the Bible, and they would quiz each other to see who got the most answers right. They would both be so close to each other it was fun to watch. They would be hard to beat—I believed they knew all the answers. I remember our preacher Ken how he preached with his visual aids. My cousin and I loved them: we would listen carefully and take notes in church while we sat by each other in church. This one day, my dad and mom bought my sister and me our first Bibles. I remember it was white and a King James Version. Still, until this day, I am not sure where they got the idea to buy us a Bible, but I sure did appreciate. I then started to read my Bible every night before I went to bed until it started to fall apart.

I remember Sharon talking about this nice Christian family that her family met and knew the B's. I asked a few questions about them, and she answered me. I remember asking if they had a boy my age. She said, "I think so, but he's not interested in girls." I said, "Oh, okay." It was not long after this Christian family moved to the area, and Roger became our preacher. I would stay at their house on the weekends, and I became close friends with their daughter named R. J. B. We would always have fun. I liked their son Robert. We were in our early teens; he melted down lead-made letters, "R," "D," and a "plus" sign. I was speechless and lost for words whenever he handed this to me. It was a very special moment in my life. My heart was touched. I will never forget that special day of my life.

JOURNEY

(AGE FOURTEEN TO THIRTY-THREE)

The most important, the best day of my life is when I was fourteen years old; in obedience to the command of our Lord Jesus Christ and in imitation of His example, I was buried with Him in baptism on February 1, 1981. Immediately thereafter, a lot of people were hugging and kissing me, but one special person I remember was P. B. whispering in my ear as she was hugging me, welcoming me to His kingdom, and the angels were rejoicing in heaven. I loved P. B. She was very special to my heart.

Remembering the "B" family, R. B. was a teenager a little older than me, the preacher's son, and Robert's brother; we were talking this one day about starting a youth group. I asked, "What's that?" "That is when teenagers get together to form a group, to go to activities such as roller-skating, ice skating, and pizza parties," R. B. replied. I remember he caught my interest, it sounded like a whole lot of fun, and that was something I would go to and do. I remember P. B., their mother, the preacher's wife, making pizza for our teenage group once a month at her house. It was so yummy!

It touched my heart being at their house and watching her love and kindness to all of us that were there. She is a special person to me and always will be. I remember going roller skating with our group this one very special time in my life. I wanted Robert to roller skate with me as the night went on. I was beginning to think he would not ask me to skate. I don't think we even talked to each other the whole night. Then the last song for the night started to play; I started to feel disappointment coming over me; then Robert skated toward me slowly and roughly, I started to smile, and a happy feeling came over me, and he asked me to skate with him. I was so excited I said yes! He took my hand in his hand, and we skated to the song "The Devil Went Down to Georgia"! I had so much peace in that moment of time, but the song ended too quickly; I wanted it to play longer. We then went about our normal Christian teenage years. I remember staying at the B's house overnight on a Friday night. The next day, on Saturday, the girls went to clean the church building. Of course, I was included; I went with P. B. and the girls to clean the church building. I remember R. J. B. complaining about having to do this, but I was excited to be cleaning God's house—that was the way I looked at it. I would be thinking of my family, my mom, dad, and sister, hoping they would take and do their part for God's house; as you see, they would attend church, drop out of church, then go back, then when I was older, they didn't attend church anymore. How special it was for the girls to be born into a preacher's family. I guess I wanted to be a preacher's daughter. This one day at the B's house, on February 13, 1983, I was sixteen years old. P. B. handed me a beautiful gift. It was a burgundy color Bible. I was lost for words. P. B. mentioned that R. J. B. had requested this gift because my Bible was falling apart. I was so excited to receive such an honor from a very special person in my life. She had written inside my Bible, "Donna, God loves you, and we do too; you are welcome in our home anytime, and God wants you to come to His home also. Read these words every day and be free." This was a very special moment of my life, and it continues to have an impact on my life. However, I do remember this one very special moment at the B's house: R. J. B. handed me a gift saying, "This was from Robert. He has been working very hard on the farm to save up money to buy this for you." It was a beautiful gold heart-shaped necklace. I remember R. J. B. putting it on my neck. I loved it. I was so happy I didn't know what to say. I did say, "Tell Robert I said thank you!" I was wondering why Robert didn't hand it to me or put it on my neck; I felt like he should have been the one to do that, and to this day, I'll never know the true story. All I know it was a very special moment in my life. I wore my special necklace all the time for many years, then the chain broke. I kept the heart in my treasure box for many years, then I took it out, wore it, then put it back. I had taken it out and placed it in a different place one day. This year 2020, I have been moving rooms in my house, going through things, throwing medals away for the junk pile, and I threw it out, not knowing this was the heart part of the necklace that Robert had given me many years ago. I tossed it in a pile of junk, thinking this was just a metal I was looking at and praying I still will find my heart; the chain has been gone a little while, now it was broken, but the heart was my treasure all these years. I am crying as I write this. I want to find what's missing in my life. I miss what stood behind my heart necklace, and my true heart has been broken over the years. Maybe I'm trying to find my heart and the special someone that I was meant to be with. I need to let go and let God bring me my heart back and my special someone to me. I looked in a bucket of old nails from the old siding that was just taken down this summer in 2020, hoping to find my heart to the necklace that Robert bought for me. I looked in the scrap siding container at the bottom, it was not there, and I checked my car trunk, hoping it would have fallen out in my trunk from the container I had it in whenever I hauled my junk metals away, but it was not there. I was hoping I would have found it knowing now that was my precious treasure I had for many years. Well, my heart is saddened it's gone to the junk pile at the scrapyard, and I'm asking myself how did I not remember this special heart. *How could I have been so careless?* I can only pray for my heart to return back to me, but I know God is healing my heart spiritually. I still may have some healing that needs to be made whole before I am given the one whom I'm supposed to be with, who needs to be made whole so, when the time comes, we can completely be whole together. Thank you, Lord, for healing me, for what has been broken inside of me—my heart, in Jesus' name, Amen, Amen, and Amen!

My church, the Mount Pleasant Church of Christ, decided to join up for a Bible bowl in Sharron, Pennsylvania. It was for teenagers, and we studied hard for it. Boy, was it ever fun? I remember getting most of the questions right and thinking about my cousin Sharon and our friend R. W. from church playing with the flashcards thinking it's not that hard if you study and put the time in reading the Bible. I was feeling pretty smart that day. It was a good experience for me and one that I will never forget. It was a team effort that I will never forget. It was so amazing all the planning and studying we all had to do to place well in the Bible bowl. We bonded with Christian families and met new people who were also Christian; it was a blast!

There have been many special moments at the B's house; they were like my family to me. I will never forget them, and as time is passing by, I pray I get to see P. B. another time in my life; she is getting older, and I don't want it to be too late. I also would like to see Robert again. This has been on my heart lately and the rest of the family too.

My heart was crushed whenever the B's moved away to Texas. In August of 1986, R. B. came back to visit all of us—we were like the family he once knew. I remember taking a picture with him, and he gave me a picture of the whole B's family. This meant so much to me, and he even wrote on the back of the picture "to Donna with Love, The B's." The picture of them was taken in July of 1986. R. B. was encouraging me to come to see their family in Texas. I wanted to see the whole family again. So I bought a plane ticket, took a vacation, went to see the B's. and R. B. worked out all the details, just like he said he would do, to make this all possible.

Finally, in 1987, I went to Texas. I was a little nervous traveling by myself, but it was all worth it. I got to see and spend time at the B's houses. The B's owned two different houses. I stayed in the house that the girls lived in with R. B. Robert lived at his parents' house, which I later in my trip got to visit with them. It seemed like this is what was missing in my life. My cousins lived down in Texas; I got to visit them too. This trip was so special to me in many ways; words just can't describe it. I enjoyed taking pictures of all of them. I helped Robert with some cooking; he was appreciative of that fact. R. B. reminded me that once I leave, I probably won't see them again for a very long time; everyone gets busy in their lives. Sadly, I knew he was right. The time went too fast. The trip was over before I realized it was time to leave. Robert wanted to talk to me before I left. After Robert asked me a question in a long about way, he was planning to live in Wyoming and wanted me to come with him; of course, that meant to be married first. Just then, God was talking to me in my mind, through my heart, and I heard His voice say, "Tell him you can't; I have things for you to do, to live out in your life." I took a few moments to talk with God; I said, "I want to say yes, but I want what you want me to do in my life. Lord, once I do all these things, will we be to-gether?" God's voice said, "You two will have separate lives but similar. All these things will come to pass after you live them out in your life." I looked at Robert, I could see a glow of light on his face, and I said, "I can't; I have things I have to do to live out in my life." Immediately, Robert respond-ed, "That's okay, I'm talking to a girl at work—she said she would marry me." The thought that went through my mind was, *Wow*! God knows what he is doing. If I would have said yes, maybe I would have embarrassed myself. I don't want to compete with anyone; I would want him to have eyes for me only. I was relieved that I said "I can't" after finding that out in that way. I was obedient to God. Well, Robert drove me to the airport in his new truck. I enjoyed the trip watching him. I even took a picture of him driving. I believe he was a little uneasy during the trip to the airport. We only spoke a few sentences to each other. I was feeling happy that I heard from God and knew what direction for my life to take. My heart was sad to be leaving, knowing I may never see the B's or Robert ever again.

Five years later, on my wedding day, November 21, 1992, I showed up at my church, the Church of Christ in Connellsville, Pennsylvania. My preacher met me at the front of the church by the front door. He said, "Donna, I want you to know that they want Father to give a blessing over the wedding." "Did you know about this?" D. B. asked. My preacher said, "Donna, you don't have to marry him, you can walk out the door, and everything will be forgotten." I thought about what he said for a few moments, and I started to consider running out the front door and not coming back. I did not know about this blessing beforehand. We were from two different beliefs. I was very upset with my mother-in-law to be for the fact that she did not ask me; she just did what she wanted to do. My mother-in-law to be started to treat me poorly, going behind my back and doing things. I just thought I could handle her without a problem. Well, on my wedding day, she went behind my back to have Father Henry, who came to give a blessing for our wedding because they were catholic. All of a sudden, I heard the Lord's voice say, "I need you to do this, meaning I need you to marry him; that is what I felt was in my heart." So then I forgave quickly; I said, "Okay, Lord, I will do this for You and marry him." Whenever I was married for the very first time at the age of twenty-six, we had a fairy tale wedding, and I was happy we were attending Church of Christ in Connellsville, Pennsylvania. J. J. L. and I lived in a very small apartment on Quarry street, we could barely move around in it, given how small it was, but we were in love and very happily married. We moved to a house that we rented on 20 Cherry Ave right before Nicholas was born. We definitely had more room to move around in. We had a very happy life.

On November 20, 1993, we had our firstborn son named Nicholas. Oh boy, he was a handful but brought us so much joy. We were happy to be parents, and we had a nice life. After Nicholas was six months old, we moved in with my parents' house while we were closing on our first house. Boy, that was hard after being married and out on our own to do what you wanted to do, like your own routine, and now you have more people in the equation trying to please. We also stayed the week at the in-laws' house. That was a different but bearable, more controlling environment than what I was used to. Well, we finally closed on our first house and moved in. It was a baby blue siding starter home and my little dollhouse. When you first glance at it, it looks like a dollhouse. I still remember how excited we were to purchase our first home together.

Nicholas was turning one year old, and we were able to have his first birthday party in our new house. I remember Nicholas had his own little cake he played with and put his face in it to take a bite. He was so cute, with white and green icing all over his face. We had our family and friends from the Church of Christ over. I made the food. I think it was hot dogs and a few side dishes then, of course, ice cream and cake. We had the party downstairs. It was a big finished basement. Everyone seemed to have a good time. Nicholas got smart toys and pushed toys for his age.

In the summer of 1995, we went on our first family vacation to Ocean City, Maryland, with the grandparents and C. D., the great-grandparent. We all had so much fun making sandcastles on the beach. We made breakfast every morning and made a few dinners in the condo the rest of the time we ate out. I remember making breakfast sandwiches, fried eggs with cheese on toast for everyone; one morning, they were good. I used to work at Wendy's fast food, where I learned to make them. Nicholas was so happy and having a blast. He loved playing in the water; of course, it was a little nerve-racking; he was one and a half years old, and I didn't want a wave coming in on the shore and carrying him away. I just loved the blue water and the walks on the beach that was so peaceful: listening to the waves, rolling into the shoreline and out again, over and over again. I almost forgot about looking for that special seashell and collecting them.

On February 25, 1996, we had our second child named Christopher, who brought us much joy; and the following summer, we went on another family vacation to Ocean City, Maryland, with C. D. and the grandparents. Nicholas and everyone had so much fun that year. We collected seashells on the beach. We spent time shopping on the boardwalk and eating kettle popcorn. It just melted in your mouth, and we watched how they made it in the big black kettles and kept stirring it a lot. All—except Christopher, who was four months old; his first tooth came in through his gums, and he was a little cranky. He rode in the stroller up and down the boardwalk. We took pictures while on the beach. Little did I know this would be our last family vacation with C. D. and the grandparents.

However, C. D. came; J. J. L., the boys, and I went for a ride to Lancaster for the day. It was nice to get away for the day and go do something; we had fun. That was my first and only time going to Lancaster.

Christopher was turning one year old, and we had his first birthday party at our blue house. We had basically the same foods, family, and church friends over. Christopher had his own little cake; he put his whole head and face all into his cake. He had red, blue, and white icing all over his face. He looked so cute. I remember Christopher got a big fire truck and some dump trucks to play in the dirt; some nice outfits to wear, mainly shorts.

Finally, on Mother's Day, May 10, 1998, our third child was born, this time named K. L. —who we prayed for would be a girl. Our prayers were answered! We got our daughter, who brought us much joy. On May 10, 1999, K. L. turned one year old. We had her birthday party upstairs, and we invited family and friends. We had pizza, cake, and ice cream. K. L. had her own little cake; she barely got any white icing on her face. She mostly got nice dresses, cute girly outfits, and baby dolls, too.

Journey

We spent the next years having birthday parties and buying diapers and pull-ups for the next ten years. We were your typical happily married couples with children. We had birthday parties at McDonald's, which were cute when they were little; Sea Base, I think, were the better parties; Chuck E. Cheeses had nice parties and once at Taco Bell. It seemed like we were always busy staying active.

The kids and I would walk to the park in the summertime and do the summer program activities they had going on. My favorite activity was making the homemade ice cream in a tin can; we would roll it all around for a long time until the ice cream was set up then it was done. We would walk to the dollar store to buy those cap guns with the red caps; the boys loved to play with them.

On Mother's Day, we used to eat at the Connellsville Golden Corral which my Aunt Sandy and Uncle Gene managed the place. My uncle Gene used to give the boys free ice cream cones every time we came in to eat. My Uncle Gene passed away; my Aunt Sandy could not manage the place, trusted in the wrong people, and lost the business. Then our favorite place to eat on Mother's Day was the Country Buffet. They had great food there like fried chicken, mashed potatoes, mac and cheese, salad bar, and a big selection of desserts.

Amen, Amen, Amen

For eight years, I was a stay-at-home mom. During this time at home with my children, I operated a daycare in my home. I watched a few children at one time plus my own; it was a challenge, but I enjoyed every minute of it. I used to watch my friend M. B.'s two children so she could go to school to become a nurse, first LPN, then RN. For the most part, the children were well behaved. We used to have fun with all the activities I used to plan. I would sell discovery toys and get free gifts for the daycare kids. I would buy some big toys for the kids to play with and tents; they had fun at my daycare. I would invite all the daycare kids to my children's birthday parties whenever we started having the birthday parties out in public places. All the children became part of my family too.

Nicholas always wanted to help me in the kitchen when he was little. He used to like to mix up box instant pudding all the time for the kids. I could tell by the smile on his face he enjoyed doing it. One time I decided to make gingerbread cookies, and Nicholas was my stirrer. Well, I put the molasses in the bowl, Nicholas was stirring away; all of a sudden, I had molasses everywhere: on the table, the floor, in the carpet; needless to say, the smell lingered for a long time in my house. I was not happy at all, and Nicholas quit helping in the kitchen. I know he felt so bad, and I told him it was okay.

Journey

After that incident, every time I asked Nicholas to help in the kitchen—he flat out refused, like if his life depended on that. He would rather play superheroes, run around the house whenever I would get busy in the kitchen. When Christopher got older, they used to play football and tackle each other. The two were always inseparable growing up: they played football, baseball, hockey together at the house. Whenever they were older, they played sports on teams. I spent a lot of time on the bleachers watching their sports games. We had traditions for the holidays. We would go to J. J. L. Aunt P. M. and Uncle H. M.'s house always two weeks before Christmas. They had a huge party and would invite all the family and friends they knew over the years. It was huge. They would make Baccala—a type of fish, octopus, and other Italian foods. So much food and deserts—you would not go hungry. When it came time to open presents, the youngest would go first; then—the oldest child, one child at a time so everyone could see what presents everyone would receive. On Christmas eve, we would go to my parents' house and have baked ham and the trimmings. When it was time to open presents, everyone opened them at the same time; it was chaotic but fun. Then on Christmas Day, we went to J. J. L.'s parents' house. We would have ham, trimmings, and Italian foods. When it was time to open presents, they opened them, one child at a time, and took turns but got the most presents. Then on Easter, we went to J. J. L.'s Aunt P. M. and Uncle H. M.'s house one week before to have dinner. They always invited the most guests. It was nice, but there were so many people it was hard to move around. Then we would go to my parent's house for lunch and J. J. L.'s parents' house for dinner on Easter Day. Eight wonderful years of marriage and all of these holiday festivities came to an end.

A perfect life I could not ask for anything else; I had it all. I was married for eight wonderful years. I have three beautiful children, and I was a stay-at-home mom. I had a little daycare going on, watching my friend's children while they worked. My one friend went to school to become a nurse. She was appreciative that I helped make this possible for her by watching her children so she could attend nursing school. I was very happy with my life, and this is what I wanted. We went to church, the Church of Christ, as a family. We were buying our house, and we had a van. We were blessed as a family.

A huge explosion happens, tearing my family apart and turning my world upside down, from a perfectly happy marriage to chaos.

TRIALS BEGIN
THE DARK AGES

It was the year 2000, and I was thirty-three years old. My life became a living nightmare. My trials had begun, and I found myself walking in the park to get peace of mind. It was a beautiful day regardless of what I was going through. I found my situation to be so overwhelming that I would walk and pray to God while walking around at Frick Park in Mount Pleasant. On occasion, I would see my friend, a nice lady who was a bank teller at my bank, mother of a friend whom I worked with at William-House, and also she was a councilwoman. She always took the time to talk to me and to see how I was doing. I always felt at peace after talking with her, and I admired her a lot. On this one occasion, after walking and praying to God, I started to leave the park, and I felt God speaking to my heart, "Wait a minute, just hang on another minute…" So I stopped in my tracks, 1 looked straight up into the sky, but instead of seeing clouds, I saw a bright light that put my whole body into a trans, and I was now having a flashback from a memory that took me back twenty years ago. I answered a telephone call from L. B.

saying she couldn't take me to church. I was devastated and threw myself on my bed. My life started to play out when I was fourteen years old. This flashback only lasted a few minutes. I came to reality. I was at the end of the parking lot of the park across from the fire station, and the person I saw was my friend standing next to me, asking me if I was alright. I said, "Yes, I just had a flashback." It was the most incredible experience I had ever had. This supernatural experience of finding the right words is hard to find. It was the most incredible day of my life, which leads us to the next chapter of this book.

However, I would like to talk about what brought me to the park in the first place, the explosion of my life. Here are the events that led up to the explosion of my life. Whenever Nicholas turned five, he was getting ready for kindergarten. Nicholas attended Y-Tots preschool, and they said how smart he was. He was saying names of dinosaurs and much more. Then the next summer, a day in August, Nicholas's grandma decided to take him shopping for school clothes. She picked up Nicholas and Christopher so they could stay overnight at her house. Nicholas was five and a half years old, and Christopher was three. The next day D. L. dropped Christopher off at the house, so they went clothes shopping for Nicholas for the first day of school. After they went shopping, D. L. dropped Nicholas off back home; as she was leaving our house, she told Nicholas, "Welcome to the big boy's world." I was thinking, *Why did she say that?* Because that was weird. And soon, I would find out.

Nicholas started kindergarten. His teacher was so nice, and she liked Nicholas. By November 1999, Nicholas wrote on a girl's name tag, ate glue, and was acting out. He became very angry. We had a teacher's meeting. She discussed how Nicholas's behavior has changed; she described it as an animal in a cage and opening the cage and the animal running wild. She said, "Donna, I believed something bad has happened to your child." I asked what she meant. She said, "I know this behavior; my son acted the same way and found out later he was inappropriately touched." I just stood there shaking my head side to side; it's so hard to grasp that something like this has happened to her son, and even worse, to think it now has happened to my son. All kinds of mixed emotions, running through my mind, wanting to make sense of all this that just happened. Nicholas's kindergarten teacher told me he needed to get some help because something bad happened to her son; she proceeded to tell me about a good therapist, handed me her telephone number, and said to give her a call.

After I arrived home from the teacher and parent meeting,

I called this counselor; she called Monsour Hospital, then they called me. On the telephone, the therapist asked me lots of questions, and in the background, she heard Nicholas acting out. "It sounds like he's having a hard time," she replied. She went on to say to bring him in for an intake, bring him to the ER. Before we went to the hospital, J. J. L. wanted to stop at Walmart first. On the way to Walmart, I asked Nicholas why he had acted out like that. Nicholas started to say that his grandmother and grandfather were fighting. From what Nicholas told me, his grandmother did something very inappropriate to him whenever he and his brother, Christopher, stayed overnight at her house in August 1999. The next day, the grandmother dropped Christopher off at our house and took Nicholas shopping for school clothes for kindergarten. She then dropped Nicholas off at my house. She said, "Welcome to the big man's world!" I had no idea what she was talking about. To respect my son's wishes, I will not be writing all of the details of what happened to him. So J. J. L. and I drove him to the hospital; he acted out the whole way there. I had bruises on my arms and legs, trying to help him. My heart was breaking; I felt so helpless in trying to help my son. While we were in the ER, Nicholas was so angry he was swearing and tearing the ER apart, tearing things down on the floor. I had to stop him. At this point, the doctors decided to admit him to the hospital. Nicholas was admitted for an overnight stay, but it turned out to be a three-day stay instead. When he was being admitted, my mother-in-law, D. L., called to talk to me. The counselor at the hospital said, "You have been through enough already; say hi, then give me the telephone." I did just that. She was screaming at the counselor, and he had to pull the phone away from his ear. My mother-in-law thought she was talking to me. I was forever grateful for his actions. After this happened, Nicholas did not talk anymore at the hospital.

It was not long after this happened that Nicholas acted out again; I had to call the ambulance. The police showed up and said, "It's best he goes to the hospital." That is what happened. They took him by ambulance to the ER, and they evaluated him. This goes on for a long period of time, with many hospital admissions. I remember being in tears on a daily basis.

It was March of 2000. At this time in my life, my son was acting out behavior-wise. I did not know why he was acting so violently. He is only six years old. He was a handful to handle. From this day on, it was like bombs going off in my house. I had to quit the daycare business in my home. Nicholas was always fighting, screaming, hitting, punching; I must say Nicholas was out of control, and he was wearing me out. This caused fighting between J. J. L. and me.

In the summertime of the year 2000, we decided to take a vacation just with our family. We only went to Bush Gardens. I thought we all needed a break; this is what was needed. We packed up our red minivan and headed for Busch Gardens. This was our very first vacation with the five of us. Only I was happy to get away. The children were ages six, four, and two. The vacation was going well. The kids seemed happy. I was happy about a lot of things like new beginnings. This is what I thought would happen when we got back from vacation. Shortly into the vacation, Nicholas was going down a water slide with his dad; Christopher and K. L. were too little. They were with me in the little pool. All of a sudden, Nicholas was screaming. He stood up too soon under the slide and busted his head open. He had to get a few stitches. That ended the water rides for Nicholas. We just left early from vacation and headed home. Once we got home and settled in from our vacation, everything seemed to be calm and peaceful.

A few days later, a bomb hit my house; this is a figure of speech. Nicholas was acting out. I knew my life was just turned upside down. The next day things were out of control: Nicholas acting out, he got so bad I had bruises on my legs, he was kicking me. I had to call the police to help contain him.

Trials Begin the Dark Ages

One day, things started to change. My husband decided not to pay our house payment. We were short of cash. It was around the holidays, he insisted on buying his mother, father, and family Christmas gifts. I was against this, but I had no say so in the matter. He could not tell his mother he had no money for gifts. We found ourselves into a snowball effect. We were getting deeper into debt. We owed a couple of house payments; other bills were getting behind; finally, we had to file Chapter Seven bankruptcy. We were able to keep our house and van. This was such an embarrassment to our family. The following year we decided to move away. We sold our house; we just came out even with our house, which was a blessing. It was too small all this time; our family had increased.

On Christmas Day in the year 2000, we had confronted J. J. L.'s parents about what Nicholas had just told us—what his grandmother had done to him. Needless to say, they had become so angry his dad's face was beet red. His dad had threatened me, so I said, "Come on, J. J. L., let's get out of here." J. J. L. would not leave at first; then he wanted to get all the presents first. I stormed off and waited in the car. Finally, after ten minutes, J. J. L. came out with a big arm full of presents stacked on top of each other, and you could barely see his head. I said, "Why didn't you leave all these presents here?" I was fuming after all of this damage she caused to our family and J. J. L. accepted her presents for the children. This made me so mad. I think this top the angriest I have ever felt in my life. Nicholas ended up in the hospital again, then again, and again, etc. Nicholas ended up in Monsour hospital a total of five to seven times, Latrobe hospital three times, Southwood hospital two times, and a respite program for a weekend. After his final hospital stay at Monsour, the doctors would not allow Nicholas to come home; he had to go to a residential facility in Washington, Pennsylvania, for a six-month program. This was my little boy separated from me. Life just wasn't fair. All of this because someone else afflicted this hurt to my son intentionally, namely his grandma, and causing pain to my family. I cried every night before I went to sleep. During this time, we moved into a bigger house. My dollhouse was too small. My family increased over the years. We had to sell our house; we just broke even, so we were back to renting a house on Bridgeport street. I would find myself walking, talking to God, as I was walking around at Frick Park. This is how I maintained my sanity going through my situation and my trials that had begun.

We were supposed to move out of Mount Pleasant, away from his family, but we only moved downtown.

Trials Begin the Dark Ages

We were finally all moved in. I was getting comfortable with the house and actually started to like living there. The children seemed to like the extra space to play in. This only lasted for a few short months. One day, Nicholas jumped up on the countertop, grabbed a small sharp knife, held it to his throat, and he said, "I'm going to kill myself!" My heart went clear down to my stomach when I saw this and heard these words come out of his little mouth. No parent wants to hear these words coming from their seven-year-old child. I started to talk to my son, talk my son out of it, and approach him at the same time; I grabbed and pulled the knife away from his little neck and out of his small hand. I was in shock at what I just witnessed; then, I have to deal with this after everything we just been through. Needless to say, this got him another hospital admission. I was so thankful that I was able to get the knife from him before he actually hurt himself. He spent some time in the hospital, the longest hospital stay he has ever had up to this point. Then it came time he was getting discharged in the late afternoon, but first, we had a family funeral luncheon to go to.

At this funeral luncheon, a dear friend of the family wanted to know where Nicholas was at. I replied, "He's in the hospital; not the hospital you think he was in; he was having issues." This was Nicholas's ninth hospital stay. Earl was a retired school teacher. He said, "I have an education in this field, I am very concerned." So I proceeded to tell him the story of what just happened to Nicholas, explaining everything that I knew at this point; also, the part about his grandma. Well, to respect my son's wishes, I will not be talking about what happened in all the details. The first words out of his mouth were, "Do you want me to talk to J. J. L., your husband?" I said, "Yes, if it will help." So E. C. and J. J. L. went into E. C.'s truck, and they talked for at least three hours. After E. C. and J. J. L. finished talking, E. C. replied, "There is something that you need to know; let's go talk in my truck." I was quietly walking to his truck, and my mind started to race around in circles, wondering what E. C. was about to tell me; what did they talk about? I get in the front passenger's seat. I take a deep breath in and leave it out, waiting on the verdict. E. C. said, "J. J. L. has something he wants to tell you." I'm thinking, *What can this possibly be?* E. C. started telling me what he and J. J. L. were talking about. E. C. then said, "J. J. L., why don't you tell her what you told me?" J. J. L. said, "Okay." J. J. L. told me how inappropriate his mother was dressed when his father was not home. J. J. L. started to say that his dad was not home. His mom came down the hallway inappropriately dressed in a nightgown and walked over to the couch where he was lying down. "Well," he said; she gave herself a different name of who she was, and it was not his mommy. To respect J. J. L., I'm not going to tell you the last thing he remembers about the situation before he could not remember anything else about what happened to him by his own mother. J. J. L. was only eight years old at this time. I was in shock again, thinking how a mother could do this to their own son and their grandchild intentionally hurting them. We are to love our children with unconditional love the same as our Father in Heaven loves us.

After this devastating talk, we left the dinner, went to pick up Nicholas at Latrobe Hospital. He was discharged, and he was coming home to me. I was so excited my son was coming home. Trying to hold my composure after learning about the story, I just found out what was a family secret for many years and that this was the first time J. J. L. talked about it to anyone. How sad that must have been for an eight-year-old boy holding that brokenness in for all these years with no one to talk to about it. My son at least had me as his mom, who I believed in fought for him, and was by his side, fighting anything that tried to come in our way of hurting my son. When we were signing papers to bring Nicholas home, it felt like eternity. Finally arriving home, words can't describe how joyful we were to have Nicholas back home with us. This time I cried tears of joy! I love my son so very much and missed him greatly.

After arriving home getting settled in with all the children, they were playing in their big bedroom, actually jumping on the mattresses that were on the floor while the beds did not get set up yet. We just moved into our house a couple of months ago. J. J. L., my husband, decided to call E. C. to talk to him on the telephone. I said, "After you finish talking to him, let me talk to him." So that is what happened; I talked to E. C. on the telephone after my husband was done talking to him. When I was talking to E. C., I said, "I think I'm going to ask the boys if they know what the name their grandmother addressed herself means." E. C. thought this was a good idea, so I did just that. He was telling me he was very concerned about J. J. L. after talking to him. Since he just talked to someone after having things bottled up inside, all this hurt from his own mother for so long. See, E. C. is a retired school teacher, so he has some experience in this field. I gave the telephone back to J. J. L.; the way I went, I was holding my breath, hoping no one knew anything and everything would be good. I went into the boys' bedroom; they were having so much fun jumping up and down, up and down on the mattresses that were placed on the floor; actually, laughing and being children. Laughing was rare these days in my family. Nicholas was enjoying being home, and Christopher was playing with his brother like old times. They did everything together, just inseparable. Minutes went by, and I popped the question, "Does anyone know what this name means?" The same name their grandmother addressed herself to their dad. To respect J. J. L., I'm not going to say the name she referred to herself as whom she was. Christopher raised his hand in the air while jumping, and he said, "I do, I do." A lump went from the back of my throat to my heart, to my stomach; I gasped for air and said, "You do—what do you mean, Christopher?" He said, "That's what grandma whispered to me in my ear when she touched me doing this…" He was doing something, then I said, "Lift your hands up, show me in the air what she did." Christopher showed me just that. To respect Christopher, I'll not be telling you what he showed me what his grandmother did to him. I said, "She did; when did she do this?" Christopher said, "When I stayed overnight, she bought Nicholas clothes for kindergarten." I said, "Thank you for telling me, son. I love you, and I'm sorry this happened to you." Christopher was five years old and only three years old when this happened. I rushed out of the boys' bedroom and ran into our bedroom; J. J. L. was still on the telephone with E. C., I flipped out, ran into my bedroom, screaming at J. J. L.,

"What is wrong with your mother: first—Nicholas's story, your story, and now Christopher's story?" I was very angry at D. L.and J. J. L. immediately told E. C. he had to go now and hang up the telephone. J. J. L. called his dad and said, "We have a problem here. Donna is saying things and making things up; I'm going to 3-0-2 her." Unbelievable! What I just heard my husband, J. J. L., says, and then he calls 9-1-1 to 3-0-2 me. I started to go crazy at this point. J. J. L. called the police, trying to 3-0-2 me. The biggest bomb ever just exploded in my house; I felt my marriage just slip out from under me, and I knew, at this point, I could not save it either. It only took minutes for the Mount Pleasant police to show up. I will never forget it was like yesterday in my mind. J. J. L.'s best friend growing up, D. S., a policeman, and the first question is what happened and the look on his face—he could not believe it either. D. S. would ask me a few questions, then he asked me the big question. Here is the biggest question of all, D. S. asked, "How much do you trust J. J. L., your husband, right now?" I answered, "Zero, I didn't trust him at all; he just went against our family." D. S., J. J. L.'s best friend and the best man at our wedding asked me: "Do you have a place to go, like a sister's house?" I said, "I have a sister." He said, "Call her; if it's okay, I will drive you to her house." I called my sister and explained what was going on. She said, "You and the kids can stay with me." Then D. S. drove us in the police vehicle to my sister's house in Scottdale, Pennsylvania. This was my family's home growing up from the time I was four years old until I was eighteen years old; then, I moved out. My sister bought our family home from my parents. I left J. J. L., we went to stay at my sister's house. My sister tried to make our lives better for the summer for all of us; we would have cookouts, go swimming, ordered pizza out a lot for the kids, and we cooked in very little. I was traumatized by what happened to my sons from their grandparent. This time in my life, we had Family-Based Therapy. We had family-based counseling that came to my sister's house. They were very helpful to the situation. There was a lot of fighting going on between my family and L.'s. Whenever I tried to take my children to fairs, the park, whenever we lived in Mount Pleasant, D. L. would scream and shout in my face. I would block her out not pay any attention to her. This went on quite a few times; then, I finally filed harassment charges against her. Then she retaliated and filed slander charges against me. Every time she screamed at me, I stood up to her and did nothing with this advice from my attorney, so I could not get in trouble for anything; therefore, if I did not say anything. I just kept on doing for my children and living the best I could under the circumstances. I had court dates scheduled for child support and scheduled counseling appointments. I could not walk around at Frick Park in Mount Pleasant anymore; I was in Scottdale; therefore, I had no vehicle to get around in. The children and I walked if we wanted to go anywhere. My life sure did change. It was turned upside down. My children and I stayed the whole summer at my sister's house.

The summer was ending; time to make decisions that would affect all of our lives. The decisions were being made where to go to live. J. J. L. was taking the kids back and forth to see their grandma—yes—the one that hurt them. Therapy sessions and it was time to leave my sister's house. All of this was overwhelming for the whole family, especially Nicholas. All these changes were hard for Nicholas, and he started to act out. Another bomb went off before we left my sister's house, and Nicholas had to be hospitalized. This time all the therapists involved made the decisions to keep Nicholas in the hospital so he could get the help he needed while, at the same time, I could organize our life.

By the end of summer, I had to make decisions on where to live and how to get some money for my family. Soon, I had to share the children with their dad. He had visitation rights, and I started to receive child support. I know what you are thinking; just keep scratching your heads; the system doesn't work the way we think it should work. Everything had to be proven in court. Well, we never did get our day in court, even to this present day. I kept reminding myself the vengeance is God's, not mine. Whatever God wanted to do in this case, I was obedient to him. I would remind myself that God loved me and Jesus was with me. I sure needed *His* strength at this point in my life. I could not even get to go to church at this time in my life; I was devastated. I love going to church. We were still attending Connellsville Church of Christ, Jeff Rowan was our preacher up to this point in my life, and now I can't go. This made me depressed and miserable. Church has always been my foundation and my rock through life; it gave me my stability no matter what was going on around me.

We moved back to the house we were renting in Mount Pleasant. The children started school in Mount Pleasant. Once again, I was able to walk around at Frick Park, talking with God about fixing my life, wondering what I was going to do next and where I was going.

Then I found a place in Jeannette, a white house; we rented the upstairs apartment out, and we stayed there for one year. I remember, one day, Nicholas was acting out, and the neighbor was helping with him. Christopher and K. L. were in the van, ready to go to J. J. L.'s house. J. J. L. and I shared the van; it was my turn to drive the kids to J. J. L.'s. I asked the neighbor to watch the kids in the van while I called J. J. L. to tell him Nicholas was acting out and we will be late. Just when I walked away from the van to do this, Christopher knocked the van out of gear, and it went down the hill. The neighbor came around the corner just in time. He pushed the van with his vehicle to the other side of the road into the neighbors stone wall. The van was stopped, and my children were safe.

I prayed to God a lot, looked for His strength to help me through all that was going on in my life. I would remind myself vengeance is His, not mine. It's God's battle, not mine, to fight. As I was dealing with all of this, I went to the hospital for some reason; then I ran into my cousin and his little girl there. He seemed to be distraught and not himself. I asked him what happened for the reason he was at the hospital. My cousin told me his daughter was sexually molested, and he was going to kill him. I said, "Steven, you don't want to take matters into your own hands." He was set on taking matters into his own hands. I tried to tell him his daughter needed him; being in jail would get him away from his daughter. He would not be useful if he was in jail. I explained to him my story and that I was letting the system handle it. I was trusting in God that the truth will come out.

Well, in therapy sessions, they always wanted to know how I was holding back. I told them the story of my cousin who took matters into his own hands, and now he could not see his daughter, and she will grow up without her dad. That just broke my heart. I was fighting for my children in the right way. I would answer people when that question would come up with; I know Jesus—that how I got my strength to keep fighting in the right way.

Thereafter, we had to take Nicholas to therapy sessions; there were many of them. I just wanted him to be better and live a good childhood.

Then we moved in with my mother and father; their house was in Connellsville, Pennsylvania. It has been eight years, and I still was living with my parents. Whenever my children were older, the boys became teenagers. They went to live with their dad and to attend Mount Pleasant School. I am trying to find a house in Mount Pleasant so we can all be together, but this is not happening. I am having trouble finding the right place for us.

After reading all of these traumatic events that took place in my life that led up to me walking and praying to God, trusting in *Him*, I keep my faith, knowing everything will work out. I did receive answers to my prayers. While I was at the park, I had an overwhelming amount of peace that was awesome, and God showed me a flashback of a time when-ever I was fourteen years old; a phone call took place that upset me; I could not go to church, I cried my heart out to God, I was reading my Bible then the most incredible super-natural event of my life happened. After coming out of this flashback at Frick Park, I remembered all of it for the first time since it happened a very long time ago, and my friend wanted to know if I was all right. I said yes. I was fine. I just had the most incredible experience. A flashback; it's a long story of whenever I was fourteen. In this next chapter, you will be able to read about this most incredible, supernatural experience of my life.

ENCOUNTER WITH GOD

God is the author and the finisher of our life. By being obedient to God's Word, His will be done in your life, not your own will. Give God all the glory for whatever you accomplish in your life, and much will be accomplished for His kingdom.

A lady drove me to the Church of Christ every Sunday and Wednesday service. I was fourteen years old when I asked Jesus in my heart as my Lord and Savior, and I was baptized on Sunday, February 1, 1981. After I was baptized, I was looking forward to a new and better life. I was expecting to experience something big to happen in my life now that I was baptized. What I did not know at that time is who I would become over the next thirty-nine years of my life. In Proverbs, chapter four, I realize this is going on in my life, walking step by step down my rightful path that God has purposed for my life. God is not angry at us for not arriving fully accomplished. We must keep pressing in, holding the plow, and continuing down our rightful path. On the following Wednesday, February 4, 1981, I received a phone call from Laura saying that she would not be able to take me to church that evening. I would not be attending Bible study because I had no ride. That evening I was very upset that I could not go to church. My mind was racing on how I was going to get to church because I did not have my driver's license. I was very disappointed and devastated that I could not attend church services. I was looking forward to going to church for the first time after I was baptized. I asked my dad if he would drive me; he loudly said *no*. I said, "Fine; I'll just read my Bible then." I went to my bedroom, slammed my door behind me, flopped on my bed, set up on my bed, and started to read Matthew 5:3-10 (KJV). I was crying my heart out to God. I kept reading down the page, I read verses 15 and 16, and then I continued reading through the book of Matthew. Then I was really drawn to Matthew 6:33 (KJV), "But seek ye first the kingdom of God, and his righteousness; and all these things shall be added unto you." I asked God questions. What am I missing in my life? What is my life going to be like? Am I always going to have disappointments my whole life? Am I ever going to be married? Am I ever going to have children? What is my purpose in my life? All these Bible women had purposes. Look at Mary; she carried and had baby Jesus. Look at Sarah; she was old and had baby Isaac; look at Lot's wife. What is my purpose? *What can I do for you, God, in this world today?* I can't even go to church. Look at all these women from way back. They all had purposes in their lives. *So what is my purpose, Lord?* You're the King of Kings and the Lord of Lords. Then I heard a voice in my room saying, "I will show you!" I looked around my room and said, "Who said that?" I flopped back on my bed; my head hit the pillow; before I knew it, my bedroom was fading away, but I was still lying on my bed. I seemed to be going in a trans. I am now in an elevator with a man who had short dark hair. His back is turned towards me; he is in the front, and I am in the back. There were many buttons; they had black numbers in the center with light around them. This man pushed one button; the elevator would make ding, the doors would open, but there was nothing there. This happened a couple of times. Then he pushed another button. The elevator would ding, the doors would open, but we stayed on the elevator, the doors closed. Then he gave me instructions; he said, "This time, I want you to keep your eyes closed." That is what I did. Whenever the elevator doors opened up, flying things came in and around me; it was a dreary feeling. I thought I was in a smelly, musty basement. I felt the wind from things flying around me. And with my eyes closed, I could see black shadows. I put my hands together as if I was praying and started to say, "Just get me out of here." I was looking upward with my eyes closed, and the man said, "Don't worry, they can't touch you." The flying things left the elevator, the elevator doors closed. The man pushed another button, it dinged, and the doors opened up. It was beautiful! The man said, "This is Animal Kingdom." I replied, "Where are the animals?" There were no animals. He did not respond back with an answer. Then I heard a stampede coming. Then this man, in the elevator with short black hair, said, "The animals are coming." Then at that moment in time, I was thinking the animals were coming into the elevator. Oh, no. Before I could even see any animals, the doors have closed. It dinged, the doors opened up. It was a beautiful place. It looked just like earth but more beautiful. The sky was a much brighter blue; the grass was a brighter color green, the trees seemed to stand stronger, nice, and straight. The leaves on top of the trees were a bold, bright color green. There was nobody there. I believe this was the New Earth mentioned in Revelations. Also, in Isaiah 65:17, "For behold, I create new heavens and a new earth; and the former shall not be remembered or come to mind." The elevator doors have closed. This man says, "We are almost there." He pushed the button, the elevator dinged, and the doors opened up. It was a beautiful sky. This man said, "We are going out this time." He took my hand as we walked out of the elevator together into the clouds. Like a spring day, it was cozy and warm, although it was a chilly day in February on earth.

Encounter With God

And now I'm lying down on my back. A huge black bird flew at me, touched my right shoulder; its beak felt cold. I said, "Oh, that bird touched me." I immediately wiped off my shoulder. I think that I am up to where the birds are. There are clouds all around me. I must be in heaven. I feel as if I am the only one here. I no longer see the man who brought me up here on the elevator. After the bird flew away, a small, still voice said, "That is so you know you were here."

All I could see was a blue sky and clouds in front of me. As I was approaching where the still small voice was, as the clouds cleared away, I could see fog and a pair of eyes looking at me; clouds were hovering around this image before my eyes. Then I heard the same voice saying, "There is someone lying next to you; he is here for his purpose. This man lives across from you on the other side." As I looked to my right, I could not see anyone; all I could see was fog. Then I realized I must be here for my purpose too. After all, I did ask God what my purpose for me in my life was and what I could do for God in this world today. God said, "This man lying beside you is looking for his special someone and only one yours truly. I am giving him a question, and he thinks that the person that has the answer to his question is his special someone and only one yours truly. I am giving you the answer to his question, but you are not his special someone yours truly." Here is the question: how do you know when your cup is half full? Here is the answer! When two Christians meet their special someone, the one they are supposed to be with, their cups are half full. And when they get married, their cups become full. I then bless their cup, and their cup will be overflowing with blessings in their marriage.

Suddenly, God moved over to the right corner, but there was no corner; I was up in heaven. I could see big hands moving around, reaching for the stars and moon. He was pulling things out of the universe, bringing them all together. It appears to be like clay that's being molded on a wheel. As I watched my Father work, I was trying to see His face. I could only see His big eyes, a slow blink, eyelids covering about half of His eyeballs. As his eyes closed and opened slowly, I could feel His love pour all over me as it radiated all through heaven. The rest of Him blended in with the clouds. God was making life. When I was writing this book, here are a few scriptures that I found.

> Then the word of the LORD came to me, saying, "Before I formed you in the womb I knew you; Before you were born I sanctified you; I ordained you a prophet to the nations." Then said I: "Ah, Lord God! Behold, I cannot speak,

for I am a youth." But the LORD said to me: "Do not say, 'I am a youth,' For you shall go to all to whom I send you, And whatever I command you, you shall speak. Do not be afraid of their faces, For I am with you to deliver you," says the LORD.

Jeremiah 1:4-8

For You formed my inward parts; You covered me in my mother's womb. I will praise You, for I am fearfully and wonderfully made; Marvelous are your works, And that my soul knows very well. My frame was not hidden from You, When I was made in secret, And skillfully wrought in the lowest parts of the earth. Your eyes saw my substance, being yet unformed. And in Your book they all were written, The days fashioned for me, When as yet there were none of them.

Psalm 139:13-16

God told me He puts half of it in one woman's womb and the other half in another woman's womb. Then when they grow up, they both ask God first to meet whom they are supposed to be with—that special someone. God will bring them together; He will make this all possible. I asked God about age. He replied, "Age does not matter. I will put half in one woman's womb, and I will hold the other half for a long time then put it in another woman's womb." When these two people ask to meet that special someone, God will make it possible. Time does not matter; all this happens in God's timing—which means one person can be much older than the other person.

Everyone has a personal purpose in life. God told me He has a purpose for everyone's life. God showed me a baby. He tells the baby its own purpose in life, then breathes it into the baby. God said, "I will show you like this." Then He breathed over me, and it felt like a gust of wind but more powerful. God showed me another live baby and said, "This person was rejected their whole life." God was telling me different things that would happen in my life. Choices I will have to make to keep on my rightful path. After hearing this, I started to question if this all was true or just a dream. I remember asking God, "How do I know these are not just words and no action with them?" God said, "Do you know your name?" I said yes. God replied, "Well, you will hear your name constantly." At the time in my life, I rarely heard my name because I only knew a few people named Donna in my whole school. I said, "If I hear my name constantly, then

I would have no choice but to believe this."

God wanted to know if I was sincere about wanting to know my purpose. I remember God asking me if I was going to be fully committed to my purpose before He showed it to me because it wasn't going to be a rose garden. It's going to take commitment, persistence, and perseverance. Once I put this into motion, I can not call it back. There will be no turning back. The choice is mine. Once I agree, I would do my very best to do my part in fulfilling my purpose in life. If I would not agree fully to committing myself to my purpose, God was not going to show it to me. I asked Him, "What do you want me to do?" He said, "Nothing, just answer questions." I remember fully committing myself. God said, "I want you to stop two evil people in this world." *Of all the people in this world, how would I know who they are? Once I know who they are, then how can I stop them?* God said, "When the time comes, you will know." I remember asking God about my children, "Will they come back to you and serve you?" The answer was—yes. I said, "Okay, I will do this for you then if my children come back to you after all this." God took action and put my purpose in motion.

God said, "Whenever you get to the place I want you to be, I will give you the key." I said, "How are You going to do that; You are up in Heaven, and I am on Earth?" God said, "When the time comes, you will see. I will lead you to a place by a friend that does not exist, but it will." God promised me after my purpose is fulfilled, that special someone, whom I'm supposed to be with, will come into my life. God said, "This was all going to happen during wartime." But it was currently peacetime. God said, "Someone will come into your life because of his job, but you will not see this person for a long time; then they come back into your life, and you both will be together." This will be my reward for doing so. I am also going to help other people by telling them to ask God first about who it is that they are supposed to be with and bring that special someone in their life. "For everyone who asks receives, and he who seeks finds, and to him who knocks it will be opened" (Mathew 7:8). Whenever two people who want to meet their one and only special someone both are on the same spiritual level, they first ask God who they are. God will make it all possible to bring them together. Whenever two people get married who are their special one and only someone, their bond is so strong and powerful that no one can break it. There is so much spiritual power that they get much accomplished for His kingdom. Your cup will be overflowing with blessings, and you will be living the abundant life.

God told me to come, so I went to see what He wanted

to show me. I looked down through the clouds at a dead man with machines hooked up to his body. God was on my right side; of course, I could not see Him. I said that man was dead. God said that not for long. God was explaining what He wanted me to do in this man's life, "I want you to blah, blah...in this man's life." I did not know what He said at this time in my life. However, years later, I have to live this out in my life as part of my purpose in life.

I asked God where the man who had brought me up there was. God said that He would show me. Just then, God appeared right in front of me! I said, "You have clothes on!" He had blue jean-like material pants on with a bell bottom and a burgundy long-sleeve button-down shirt. God said, "I like clothes." I started to follow Him. He looked like an image of a man, but He was a spirit being. We were walking down a hallway, turned right, into a room. I was walking in God's house in heaven. All I could see was a white and blue sky that went on and on. There was no ending to the sky. I felt like I was going to float away. In the middle of the never-ending skies, there was Jesus sitting on His throne. In a blink of an eye, I was at His throne in God's presence. God was on my right. The power of God's presence is like gravity, like standing on the floor, but there was no floor. I said, "This doesn't look like the man who brought me up here; this man has long hair." Then God said, "He can look any way He wants because He is Jesus, but He is choosing to look the way I, His Father, want Him to look." As God was speaking, He's looking at Jesus. I was looking at Jesus; He was listening carefully to God's words. God is well pleased with Jesus. After God was done speaking, Jesus bent slightly over to His right side and reached down with His right hand. It seemed like He was picking paper off the floor, but His hand went straight down through heaven, and it reached down to the people. I was questioning what He was doing, and God replied, "He was moving a person, who was stuck in their life, in a different direction so they can move forward with their life." God was explaining to me that He cares for people by giving them a pat on the back and wiping their tears away when they are crying. Basically, He was telling me how He loves and cares for us. God explained to Jesus that we were going to start the movie. God wanted Jesus to come to join us at some point. I was following God out of the throne room when I fell down below a doorway, gripping tightly, holding on to the bottom edge. I could see God's back getting further from me as He was walking away. God proceeded back down the hallway to where we started from. I could no longer see Him. I was wondering, surmising He would come back for me. The power of His presence was broken when I fell, and I was holding on to the bottom edge of the doorway. I felt like I was floating backward. I turned to my right, looked behind me, and I could see a blue sky that goes on and on like ripples of deep blue ocean waves. Jesus was sitting on His throne in the middle of the ripples of deep blue ocean waves, but we were up high in the sky, and at a distance, I could see white clouds. Just then, God came back to get me. He said to get up. I said that I couldn't. Again, He said, "Get up." I said, "I can't." Then God said, "Just get up." I said, "Okay, here it goes." I pushed myself down against the edge of the doorway and went up. I was now in His presence. Within a blink of an eye, I was following God back down the hallway, where we started from. Currently, as I'm writing this, this part reminds me of this scripture that I found.

> Then Jesus said to them, "When you lift up the Son of Man, then you will know that I am He, and that I do nothing of Myself; but as my Father hath taught Me, I speak these things. And He who sent Me is with Me. The Father has not left Me alone, for I always do those things that please Him."
>
> **John 8:28-29**

Amen, Amen, Amen

God asked me, "What goes with a movie?" I said, "Popcorn." He said, "I'm going to give you something like popcorn, but it is not popcorn." I could see the light inside a popcorn machine and a big silver scoop. God opened the door and scooped out this "something like popcorn," then handed it to me. It was good. I was sitting on a couch, so I thought. God was showing me different parts of my life; as a movie was playing in my mind, everything was running together. As I was walking down a path, it was like I was back on earth. I could see trees, green grass, and green street signs with white letters, but I could not make out the words. As I approached the street signs, I could see my future play out in front of me. As I would continue to walk down my path, each time I would come to a sign, I would see another part of my future play out. As I was walking, it started to get dark. I tried to hurry to get to the end of my destination so I could get back home before it got too dark. After God showed me my life and my purpose was fulfilled, I remember saying, "Is that it? You brought me all this way, and that is it?" I asked, "Why can't justice be done?" I was no longer walking on my path; I was watching the movie of my future playing in my mind. It started with questions on a stand in the courtroom; the truth was coming out. Then another person took the stand; they were lying; the judge knew this and became angry. The judge was asking about a lie detector test taken. The judge said, "I want everyone subpoenaed who has anything to do with this case." My friend was subpoenaed, but he couldn't be found. I told the courts to check where his brother lives because that was where he was supposed to go. My friend was found, and then he testifies on my children's behalf. This person was a witness to their behaviors. I asked him, "Where is so and so?" He said, "She left me." My children testify on the stand, but I remember being minus one child. A counselor and a doctor testifies; also, a court advocate is there supporting us. Near the end of the trial, my attorney approaches me; he says, "I need more money to finish the trial." The judge orders a recess. I call up my male friend and tell him my situation. He brings me around a thousand dollars. The trial is back in session. During court, a man of the law stands up and says, "I will do it." I am not sure what this was about at this time. Then we were able to finish the trial. The judge rules in my favor.

The first evil person I was to stop according to my purpose—she gets community service, has to buy a house for my children and me because she ruined our marriage and broke up our home. The judge rules the amount be paid for a house would be worth two hundred and fifty thousand dollars. After this was all over, I was kneeling on the courtroom floor, hugging my children and praising God. I remember God saying that the person who stands up and helps me with my children will be greatly blessed. I remember buying a house, paying off bills, and buying a man a brand new motorbike. This man is the one who hears God's voice and helps me out. To show my appreciation for everyone who helped my children and me out, I took everyone to Disney to celebrate our victory. I give God all the thanks, praise, and all the glory; forever Amen.

After the movie was done playing, Jesus was in the room. He was holding a wooden treasure box that was closed. Jesus said, "Before you go, I want you to have this." He opened the box, and it was filled with treasures, such as diamonds, silver, gold, jewelry, and a lot of bling. Jesus said, "If you take this box, you won't have Me; but if you choose Me, you will have everything." And I said, "I choose you, Jesus; You are my treasure." God said, "It's time to go back." I wanted to stay in heaven. God said, "No, you must go back; you have to grow up and live out your life so all of this will happen." There was so much love and peace; it was indescribable.

Spiritually, I was holding on to God. God showed me a time dial of my life. This time dial looked like a big clock with Roman numeral numbers on it. It also had words that were events of my future. As the dial or hands moved to an event, that event, that is my future, would become my present and would play out in my real life. God showed me my life is like putting a puzzle together. Each piece represents an event of my future. As the event happens in my life, it's like adding another piece to the puzzle. Once the last puzzle piece is in place, the big picture will be revealed. Also, God showed me that we are Christian soldiers marching in His army. We looked like little black ants marching, and everything around us was orange. This reminds me of the song "Onward Christians Soldiers."

At approximately 8:45 p.m., I woke up. It was around four hours later since I got the call from Laura that she was not able to pick me up for church. After waking up, my first thoughts were that I was dreaming. Then I said, "No, that was too real to be a dream." Then I got up out of bed, ran out of my room to find my parents. I had to tell them about my experience. I first checked the living room; they were not there. I found them in the kitchen. Zealously, I was trying to tell them about my experience. My dad said, "Oh, you were dreaming." I said *no. No, it was so real.* Trying to convince my Dad it was real and not a dream, I went back into my bedroom; I walked over to my closet; on the door there, I had a map of the United States of America. I followed the instructions I received from God when I was up in heaven that someone lives on the other side of me from where I live. I found Pennsylvania, which is where I live; with my finger, I went the whole way across the map; I found the state of California. I thought, *Oh, that person is from California.* I circled the state of California. Once I realized this person was from California, I wanted to know how I was going to give him the answer to his question when I am fourteen years old and I have no way of getting from Pennsylvania to California. I said to myself, *This is impossible; maybe this was a dream after all.* I thought the only way would be to take an airplane or by telephone; then I realized I didn't even know this person; so, I could not even do that. That was the only form of communication when I was fourteen years old.

I knew this was an amazing love story. God said, "All this will come to pass." And I will be living the abundant life that He has planned for me. In John 14:6, it says, "Jesus said to him, 'I am the way, the truth, and the life. No one comes to the Father, except through Me.'"

I was very excited about all of this. I was looking for scripture, being excited about the things of the Lord. I found this one, "We are confident, yes, well pleased rather be absent from the body and to be present with the Lord" (2 Corinthians 5:8).

John 14:11 says, "Believe Me that I am in the Father

and the Father in Me, or else believe Me for the sake of the works themselves."

> Jesus answered and said to him, "If any-one loves Me, he will keep My word; and My Father will love him, and We will come to him and make Our home with him. He who does not love Me does not keep My words; and the word which you hear is not Mine but the Father's who sent Me."

John 14:23-24

Psalm 27:4 says, "One thing I have desired of the Lord, That will I seek: That I may dwell in the house of the Lord All the days of my life, To behold the beauty of the Lord, And to inquire in his temple."

God gave me all these promises for my life. He said, "They will happen." I am believing and trusting in God that these promises will happen in my life. At this time, I am forty-nine years old writing this chapter of my book; this all happened a long time ago, but they are still unfolding in my life. I'm asking God questions about my life, and I am trusting God in every situation that I will receive the answers that I need. Philippians 4:19-20 says, "And my God shall supply all your need according to His riches in glory by Christ Jesus. Now to our God and Father be glory forever and ever. Amen."

Remember these things as you read, and I go into the next chapter of my book talking about the Holy Spirit leading us in our lives to make the right decisions in our life.

BREWING THE HOLY SPIRIT IN YOUR LIFE

Then Peter said to them, "Repent, and let every one of you be baptized in the name of Jesus Christ for the remission of sins; and you shall receive the gift of the Holy Spirit. Verse 39, For the promise is to you and to your children, and to all who are afar off, as many as the Lord our God will call."

Acts 2:38-39

Romans 5:5 says, "Now hope does not disappoint, because the love of God has been poured out in our hearts by the Holy Spirit who was given to us."

Upon our spiritual life, we encounter spiritual visions and dreams that God placed in our life. Within visions and dreams are spiritual encounters that we can experience through the Holy Spirit to guide us down our rightful path God has planned for us. To go from natural to the supernatural, visions are made for us to receive a word from God; dreams are given for us to receive our calling. Here is a poem to go with, what we will be talking about.

ONE NIGHT IN A DREAM

I came home from work that night and went to bed that night.

Went to sleep and had a dream of someone talking to me.

The voice: "Donna, tell me please, what shirt you were wearing that day."

I answered him and said the red one I was wearing that day.

And that night, I truly woke up and phoned to my surprise.

There was no one there that I might see when I opened up my eyes.

Went to sleep once again, and what else did I see?

My friend W. D. was standing next to me upon this dream.

Then a lady was sitting down playing a game?

W. D. said, "Sure, I'll play this game; I'll take a chance."

And she threw the dice and hit the end of the table.

I then woke up from the dream.

To my surprise, there was nothing that I have seen.
Went back to sleep and noticed this night had turned to day.

Created by Roberto Feliciano
Inspired by Donna Defelice

Let me explain how this poem came about one night in a

dream. On Saturday, December 19, 2015, I was half asleep and half awake when a voice said, "Donna, what shirt are you going to wear to church? I really need to know what shirt you are going to wear." I said, "My red one with the ruffle." Realizing I just answered someone in my bedroom, I immediately woke up; I did not see anyone, so I closed my eyes. In an instant, like a blink of an eye, I could see myself standing straight and tall with my red shirt on. I see my friend W. D. standing in front of me, then taking a few steps away to my left; then he was standing in front of a lady that is on my right a distance away. She was sitting further away at a distance, then W. D. standing in front of her. She had white and blonde hair with big brown glasses. She quickly turned her head away, and I could not see her face. It looked like this lady was playing a game. W. D. said, "I want to play chancy with you." I said, "I never heard it called chancy before. Really, W. D., chancy?" Then I could see her shaking something, and it rolled on the table, and it made a sound then I woke up. I said, "Wow, that was real." It is Sunday, December 20, 2015.

Psalm 16:11 (KJV), "Thou wilt shew me the path of life: in thy presence is fullness of joy; at thy right hand there are pleasures for evermore."

Let me take you to a prior event in November. In my

dream, I went to see my friend W. D. I looked in this room, and I could see a huge bed with two lumps, like the blink of an eye. My friend was standing beside me outside this bedroom. I started to say, "I need you to do something that was very important." W. D. said, "Okay, I will do this." I don't know what the very important thing was that I said. All I remember that W. D. was not mad at me for waking him up to tell him this. He was in agreement.

Romans 8:28 (KJV), "And we know that all things work together for good to them that love God, to them who are the called according to his purpose."

On Saturday, December 5, 2015, my church was having The Return to Bethlehem Tour. I was part of the medical team that night. I decided to walk through it with my friend, who was also on the team. Low and behold, my friend W. D. was our tour guide. He was going by the name of Luke. During the tour, we passed the bread and fish, and we turned around to see and hear about leather. Just then, while I was standing still, I felt a magnet pulling at my lower back on my right side; I could feel power. I was saying in my mind, *I felt that!* Quickly, I turned around to see what I felt with a surprise—W. D. was standing close by me but was not touching me. I believe this was a sign of God's love and power in which God wanted me to experience.

Brewing the Holy Spirit in Your Life

Do all things without complaining and disputing, that you may become blameless and harmless, children of God without fault in the midst of a crooked and perverse generation, among whom you shine as lights in the world, holding fast the word of life, so that I may rejoice in the day of Christ that I have not run in vain or labored in vain.

Philippians 2:14-16

Revelation 7:12 (KJV), "Saying, Amen: Blessing, and glory, and wisdom, and thanksgiving, and honour, and power, and might, be unto our God for ever and ever. Amen."

Here are some poems to go with, what we will be talking about.

FIND THE WAY

To find the way we see the light within our darkest day.

And when the day starts growing dim, we tend to lose our way.

We found a way we hold so dear; that's deep within our hearts.

The love God has for us—it will never part.

Created by Roberto Feliciano
Inspired by The Holy Spirit

GOD'S VISION IN MY DREAM

The dream I had—became so clear, and knowing why I am here.

To save a life within my dream and help this soul to be set free!

God brings hope within our pain when stress and sorrow come our way.

He helps us on how to win the fight upon our days that turn to night.

And knowing this on what I must do—to see this life to make it through.

I followed Him with love and grace; He guided me on my way.

He helped me to see it through; in Him, my life remains.

Created by Roberto Feliciano
Inspired by The Holy Spirit

WALKING IN LIFE'S JOURNEY

Walking in life's journey, life brings us problems around the way;

Life gives us struggles each day.

Life makes a promise for us to receive; the grace of His mercy for us to free.

Life was made for us to stand; life was given in His mighty hand.

Life we know on what we face within our trials upon this day.

Life was given for us to receive the joy of His love and the peace that we need!

As we walk in life's journey, we are faced with hard times such as stress, depression, and Anxiety—these patterns can lead to suicidal behavior.

But when we are led by the spirit, God makes way for us to fight this behavior.

Created by Roberto Feliciano
Inspired by The Holy Spirit

THE YEAR 1973

As we were walking home that night, something I saw was a terrible fright:

This man got shot in front of me; gave me chills. I could not sleep!

My mother heard me started to cry, came to my room,

and sat beside me;

She held my hand till I fell asleep.

Created by Roberto Feliciano

THE YEAR 1988

As I was heading straight to work, something happened to me.

That night really hurt; I was held up by this guy—he nearly took my life!

And as I saw my life go by, I thought this day I was going to die!

Life for me was really hard, with so much pain and many scars.

Pain and suffering came my way.

Created by Roberto Feliciano

LET US

Let us create a whole new life within the image of our Lord Christ!

Let us begin a whole new day upon our knees as we pray!

Brewing the Holy Spirit in Your Life

Let us begin to make it known: of His great love, we are made whole!

Let us create a whole new song as we praise and sing along!

Let us begin to find a way to what we do when we pray!

Let us create a joyful sound, living in peace in what we found!

Created by Roberto Feliciano

Our life is a gift from God that is so precious; it's our treasure to be treasured. In return, what we make out of our life is our gift to God. God will treasure our life. We are God's treasure. I will be talking more about our treasure in the next chapter of my book. For now, I would like to discuss a vision God shared with me in a dream. It's about our life in a pot and brewing the Holy Spirit in our life. God said, "Donna, it goes like this." I'm in a dream: there is a huge black kettle or pot with fire burning under this pot. God is stirring up whatever is in this pot with a huge wooden paddle. My question is, what is wrong with people's lives? God answered, "It is like this putting all the right ingredients in your life, and if you get too many wrong ingredients in your life, it will get too hot, combustive, and explode." This is what makes people want to commit suicide. We need to brew

79

the Holy Spirit in our lives by putting the right ingredients in our life. People become angry with their life and take it for one reason or another. I know some people in my life who committed suicide, and numbers are growing. It's time to stop this behavior. If you are reading my book and the thought has crossed your mind, *stop*—don't do it. God loves you, and the Holy Spirit never leaves you. Cry out to God and ask Jesus to help you. Jesus cares for you, and you are not alone. Whenever I was telling my pray partner about this part of my book, what God showed me about the big black kettle pot, this is what he told me. The pot represents God; the fire, in which He heats the pot up as it's being prepared, represents Christ. The water represents life, the seasonings represent God's anointing, and the flavoring represents the Holy Spirit. The right ingredients to add to your pot are love, peace, joy, happiness, tranquility, and forgiveness. By doing so, you are choosing life over death. The wrong ingredient is sin. As the pot is heating up, you are killing the germs, like anxiety, stress, and unforgiving. As the germs are being killed, you are surrendering your life to God, and you'll have forgiveness.

Whenever I was talking to my prayer partner and telling him about what happened in my dreams, that is when he came up with these poems, the ones that we just read, and they are listed above. He said, "The Holy Spirit inspired me to write these poems. I pray that you, too, will be inspired after reading my book."

Let me take you back in my story whenever Nicholas grabs a knife to his throat. I thank God to this day that I have my son with me today on this earth, and he did not do it; also, I was able to intervene in that situation. That was the hardest thing ever so far as a parent that I had to face and make a quick decision on the spot. There are many situations out there today where no one could intervene or did not even see it coming. We can take a look at a group of a few different people. First, we have people who don't believe in God at all, which is very heartbreaking to me. This would be a category where one of my co-workers hung himself in his apartment, and no one could see it coming. A friend at work and I try to witness to him about Jesus on a few different occasions but with no success. After taking his own life, we were all torn inside and felt very helpless. My friend at work said to me, "We try to witness to him; he just did not want to hear it." We did what God wanted us to do. She did comfort me with her words. Second, we have people who believe in God. A dear friend of mine who was a Christian, I would take globs to her house and visit with her. She so much enjoyed our visits and eating chocolate globs. She moved a few times, and we lost contact. I find out later after the fact that she overdosed on Tylenol. I was devastated. I miss my friend dearly. We cannot assume someone will not commit suicide when they appear to know the Lord; only God truly knows a person's heart. The truth is we must always add the right ingredients in our life to brew the Holy Spirit. And third, someone may think there is no way out. I met a dear person through his job, whose paths had crossed in life, who helped me in my situation many years ago: one of my trials that I was going through with Nicholas when he was younger. He has done his job well on this one day; D. Z. became in a situation where he was the one in authority with officers under him but, intimidated by peer pressure, could not stop what was happening. Things began to spin out of control: a couple of officers began to beat a person, who they thought was on drugs, with their clubs, but after a while—they went to the hospital to find out this person had an allergic reaction to medication. D. Z. stayed with this person for a few hours to comfort him to make sure he was all right. I know this story because this person is my fourth cousin. Arrogating the papers came in the mail of one being sued. The whole department and city would probably look down on this person who was in authority. The pressure was too much, and he shot himself in the heart. This was out of character for D. Z.

He was a very caring person. He would ask me if I had goals in my life. This was important to him. Why did these terrible things happen to my friends? I'm sure you know someone or heard about someone who committed suicide. We may never know the answers to our questions. My friend, we need to put a stop to this trend. *Stop*! If you are thinking about doing such a thing as this, please, stop! I know a Comforter—His name is Jesus. Invite Him into your heart today. I know God: He is your Father, the Almighty One, the Most Holy One, and He loves you. God is love; that all He knows is love. Jesus cares for you. Accept Jesus Christ as your Lord and Savior!

I want to take this time for you to invite Jesus into your heart. Make Him ruler of your heart. Ask for forgiveness of your sins. Your Word, dear Lord God, says whosoever calls upon the name of Lord—shall be *saved*! In the name of Jesus. You must believe in Jesus Christ, the Son of the living God. Say, I believe. I believe Jesus died for my sins (for me) that He was buried and raised from the dead. Confess with your mouth, right now, that Jesus Christ is the Lord of my life. I receive by faith eternal life into my spirit; thank you, Lord, for saving my soul. I now have Jesus Christ dwelling in me. I am saved, I am born again, I am a new creation. *Halleluyah*! Now that you have said these words, you are now a "born again" Christian. Once you find a church to attend, you can be buried with Jesus in baptism.

Praise God! Thank you, Lord Jesus, for coming into my life. Thank you, K. B., and all my family I have at Word of Life. I love my pastors; thank you, Pastor Tom. I want to take this time to thank you for all your teachings feeding God's Word. My faith has grown eminent since I first attended Word of Life ministries back in August 2001. Romans 10:17, "So then faith comes by hearing, and hearing by the word of God." This is the place where God wanted me to be. God led me here through an encounter I had with Him when I was fourteen years old.

Chapter Four describes the events taking place whenever I was up in heaven spiritually in God's house, my Father's house. God truly loves you and me. My book is about my purpose of God's will for my life being fulfilled through the Holy Spirit by the grace of God.

Whoever is reading this book, with all that being said thus far, let us continue in the Holy Spirit as we live out our lives. Are you brewing the Holy Spirit as you stirring your pot, adding ingredients into your life? Let all the right ingredients be added to your life. God can handle anything in your life; there is no problem bigger than God. God loves you so much. Give Him a chance, surrender your life to Him, ask

Him for forgiveness, and accept Jesus into your life as your Lord and Savior. There will be no regrets. What God has done in my life, also He will do for you. God is no respecter of persons.

Ask God to soften your heart; life may have taken a toll on you, and you may have a hardened heart. This is vital in hearing God's voice in your life and being led by the Holy Spirit. We need to become spiritually sensitive to the leading of the Holy Spirit, hearing God's voice, knowing right from wrong, and making right decisions in your life. This way, you will be able to make better decisions as you are on your life's journey going down your rightful path that God has planned for your life. Let God's will for your life be done, not your own will. Being obedient to God's voice will take you on a supernatural adventure that you can't even wrap your mind around it; a life's journey, one that you will have joy, peace, happiness, and a long-lived one. There can be no regrets; only enjoy the abundant life God has promised you. Whenever you choose Jesus in your life, you have everything. Jesus is our treasure, which brings me to the next chapter.

TREASURE THE GOLD AGE

We are God's treasure. God loved us first. Jesus was obedient to God's word and died for us; our sins were nailed to the cross. This is how much God loved us, and Jesus loved His Father. We must hear, believe, repent, confess, and be baptized. That is hearing God's word getting it inside of you by thinking about what you heard. Read His word for yourself so you will know God's truths and won't believe a lie. Then your faith will begin to grow, and you will believe only God's word, the truth. You will start building a relationship with God by praying to Him every time you can throughout the day. Then you find out you will be meditating on His word, praying more often, understanding of His word starts to flow through you. Whenever you want to know something, just ask God; if it is His will, He will reveal it to you, then you will understand it. But if not, that's okay; you are not going to understand everything; we don't need to understand—just be obedient to God's word. Then you will clearly see what you need to repent of; just start repenting whatever is on your heart and come to your mind by praying to God to ask Him to forgive you of your sins. Start confessing what you have read God's word, now what you believe that Jesus is the Son of God, He came, was born, and His mother was a virgin. He died for you, and He was nailed to the cross and then arose off the cross, ascended back to His Father in heaven, and now lives within us; He goes with us everywhere we go. The first opportunity you get to be buried in the water of baptism with Jesus—He is waiting for you this very minute. Please don't let this opportunity pass you by. As you can see, life is just too short, and we are not promised tomorrow. Tomorrow just might be too late. Come for you must live in the present. This is my friend, His name is Jesus, and He is the best treasure you will ever have and will find. Please will you make Him Lord and your personal Savior today!

By reading His word—the Bible, you will see there is so much love in there for us and more than this world can not contain.

> Again, the kingdom of heaven is like unto a merchant man, seeking goodly pearls: Who, when he had found one pearl of great price, went and sold all that he had, and bought it.

Matthew 13:45-46 (KJV)

By reading God's Word, we can read so many parables that teach us in our lives today what we are to do. We are to get rid of all the distractions in our life by selling what we have, do what is the most important, pick up our cross, and follow Him. Jesus is our pearl, our special treasure.

Looking back when I had my encounter with God at age fourteen, and at the end, whenever it was time to come back home, Jesus said to me, "Before you go, I want to give you something." And in His arms, He was holding a big brown wooden treasure box; there was jewelry, diamonds filled to the top, pearl necklaces, and once He opened it, I believe I saw some money too. Jesus said I could take this box with me, or I could pick Him and have everything. I said, "I want You, Jesus! You're my everything."

Some people find treasures in this life; if you really look, we have treasures all around us. One person might think of finding a shiny rock; they found some treasure, or diamonds, etc. I know a few elderly people who find their pictures of their families to be their treasures. Also, we can look at something as garbage to us, and it is a treasure to someone else in their life. Whatever the case may be, choosing Jesus is the best treasure of all; you will have everything you will ever need.

We have Jesus inside of us; oh, yes, what a treasure we have!

But we have this treasure in earthen vessels, that the excellence of the

power may be of God and not of us.
We are hard-pressed on every side, yet
not crushed; we are perplexed, but not
in despair; persecuted, but not forsak-
en; struck down, but not destroyed—
always carrying about in the body the
dying of the Lord Jesus, that the life
of Jesus also may be manifested in our
body. For we who live are always delivered to death for Jesus' sake, that
the life of Jesus also may be manifested in our mortal flesh. So then death
is working in us, but life in you. And
since we have the same spirit of faith,
according to what is written, "I believed
and therefore I spoke," we also believe
and therefore speak, knowing that He
who raised up the Lord Jesus will also
raise us up with Jesus, and will present
us with you. For all things are for your
sakes, that grace, having spread through
the many, may cause thanksgiving to
abound to the glory of God. Therefore
we do not lose heart. Even though our
outward man is perishing, yet the inward man is being renewed day by day.
For our light affliction, which is but for
a moment, is working for us a far more
exceeding and eternal weight of glory,
while we do not look at things which

Treasure the Gold Age

are seen, but at the things which are not seen. For the things which are seen are temporary, but the things which are not seen are eternal.

2 Corinthians 4:7-18

There is scripture as I was reading my Bible that I thought would fit right here in my book. While we are going through life and down the path that God has laid out before us, we need to lay up our treasures in heaven.

Do not lay up for yourselves treasures on earth, where moth and rust destroy and where thieves break in and steal; but lay up for yourselves treasures in heaven, where neither moth nor rust destroys and where thieves do not break in and steal. For where your treasure is, there your heart will be also.

Matthew 6:19-21

I'm thinking of when I'm giving God my tithe. One time, I can remember God letting me know that this was the only problem he had with me—was not giving Him all the tithe. I try really hard to give back to God what's His. I find myself negotiating with God over giving the tithe. There are times I'm on track giving, and my life is so blessed. Then a big change happens in my life, and everything gets affected. Then I'm back negotiating with God that I'm short and what I can give him on a regular basis until I organize my finances and get back on track with my tithe. This is what I call having a relationship with my Father in heaven, and my life has been blessed. I trust God with everything in my life, and if He wants me to know something, he reveals it to me. Jesus makes our relationship possible with our Father in heaven. Jesus is the reason for everything in our lives.

In Matthew 19:21, "Jesus said to him, 'If you want to be perfect, go, sell what you have and give to the poor, and you will have treasure in heaven; and come, follow Me.'"

Just like in my story at the beginning of my journey in life, I had a heart pendant, which was my treasure for thirty-plus years, I kept in a special place. Then I threw it out this one day, not recognizing this was my shining special treasure for all these years. My friends, Jesus is our treasure: hang on to Him for your entire life; until you take your last breath, don't let go or toss Him out of your life, not ever.

Just like seashells are so special and unique, and they are our treasure whenever we go to the beach, and we try to find the special ones that stand out to us. We are *God's* treasure just like the seashells are special and unique—they are all different; God just reaches His hands in the ocean and scoops us up and holds us there in the palm of His hands. God loves you so much. We are so important to *Him* that He takes time out of *His* busy work to care, admire our uniqueness, and just love on us. *God* hears your cries and prayers. Remember in my story: I was crying and very upset that I could not go to church. *God* heard me, took His time out of what *He* was doing to spend hours with me on a Wednesday evening, February 4, 1981, to show me my future and purpose on this earth—my life's journey. So as you can see, this is one story like one seashell, and so many more stories and seashells are out there. Let's share our stories that God put on our hearts and made them part of our life; I want to encourage you so you can encourage someone else who may be going through the same things or very similar to your story.

> Yes, if you cry out for discernment, And lift up your voice for understanding, If you seek her as silver, And search for her as for hidden treasures; Then you will understand the fear of the Lord, And find the knowledge of God.

Proverbs 2:3-5

Remembering, whenever my children were young, they would give me treasures, like their finger-painted handprints, drawings of their best artwork, and just little gifts that mean a lot to me. If you have children, then you know what I mean. We may keep most of these treasures the rest of our lives, or something may happen to them out of our control: when they are lost or destroyed somehow. Well, my point is although these are our special treasures; however, we are to chose Jesus as our treasure far above all of these other treasures in our life, guard and protect so nothing will happen to lose Him from your life. Always choose Jesus in every situation of your life.

Since I have remembered this vision in the year 2001 and looking over my life, yes, I have sinned, I had distractions in my life, I wasn't seeking *God's* kingdom first in my life, and it goes on and on. So I repent and move forward, keep making the right decisions in my life, and going down the rightful path God's will for my life, not my will to be done. I have come to the conclusion that this is ongoing, and I have not yet arrived at the abundant life God has promised us. There is always room for growing spiritually and improvements in my life. I can tell you by choosing Jesus as my Lord and Savior on a regular basis, I do have joy, peace, and my faith has grown over the years in my life. Since I had chosen Jesus many years ago, *He* has been my treasure like a pearl in the parable, and I surely would not want to lose *Him* ever! My faith continues to grow on my journey throughout my life as we read the next chapter.

REBUILDING MY LIFE
(AGE THIRTY-FOUR TO THE PRESENT)

> You are the light of the world. A city that is set on a hill cannot be hidden. Nor do they light a lamp and put it under a basket, but on a lamp stand, and it gives light to all who are in the house. Let your light so shine before men, that they may see your good works and glorify your Father in heaven.
>
> **Mathew 5:14-16**

Well, we moved during this time to Jeanette, Pennsylvania; to be honest, I was scared for the first time in my life. I met my neighbor John. He was so nice to my kids and me. I asked him right away if there was a church nearby. He replied, "Yes, my friend Brian attends the Word of Life just about ten minutes from here; I will tell him, and he will take you." At this time, J. J. L. and I had to share our red van. Whenever he had visitation, he got the van. Whenever the kids were with me, I had the van. That is what happened; Brian became my friend and picked me up for church. I then attended the Word of Life at the end of August of 2001. Brian would visit me, bring cookies for the kids, and K. L. would play with his daughters, who were around the same age. Whenever I could not get Christopher picked up from kindergarten a half-day because K. L. was taking a nap or it was raining outside, I would call Brian up on his cell phone; he would leave whatever job he was doing to go to the school to pick Christopher up and bring him home for me. I was forever thankful for Brian helping me out. I would make sloppy joe sandwiches whenever he came with the girls to visit. Then one day, he stopped coming over, and he ran off and got married. I was a single mother of three beautiful children who were having behavioral issues and being wild. Who can blame them whenever the adult acts in such a way to harm my children, then gets away with it, then to call me crazy, and call Youth Services on me trying to say I was the unfit parent. I had Youth Services called on me a total of ten times from the grandma. She kept on insisting I was crazy, and she wanted to raise my children at her house with their father and have me put away. Well, that was far from the truth, and I prayed harder that the truth would come out. Well, everyone meant well that was trying to help my little boy out. We still had family base counseling for that year we lived in Jeanette. They were very helpful in getting me on my own two feet. Then one day, I was getting everyone ready in the van to take the kids to their dad for visitation. Well, Nicholas started to act up outside and would not get in the van to go to his dad's house. I had to call him to say I would be late. Nicholas didn't want to come. I asked neighbor R. Y. to watch the two kids in the van. She was on the outside of the van in the doorway of the passenger's side. I went to go call J. J. L. on the house phone, I did not get far I heard a scream—it was R. Y.; Christopher came up to the front of the van and knocked the van out of gear; the van was going down a big hill, and the neighbor J. Y. came around the corner; just in time he pushed the van across the road into the other neighbors' wall and stopped the van. Thank you, Lord, for protecting Christopher and K. L., and thank you, Lord, for J. Y.'s quick reactions. I did not even care about the van anymore; it was all wrecked up. Nicholas straightened up, and I called J. J. L., and he got a ride to come to get the kids for his visitation. While bombs were going off in my house, as a figure of speech, the children were acting out; there were big explosions, planes crashed into the twin towers in New York City, the buildings fell; in Shanksville, a plane crashed to the ground—they were all terrorist attacks. My heart was very heavy and saddened during this horrifying time. My condolence goes out to the families of their loved ones who were lost. They will not be forgotten. Praying for healing for all the families that were affected by these tragedies. There were so many people who lost their lives on September 11, 2001.

So now the kids and I are back walking everywhere again, picking Chris up from half a day kindergarten and grocery shopping. I started to attend a program to help me get back into the work field since I have been out for eight years. The program was called Westmoreland Human Opportunities. They helped me, and by finishing the program, I would receive money toward a car and some business-like clothes and shoes. I enjoyed the program. I gained my confidence that I needed to get a job. It worked in no time at all. I had gotten a job sometime in January of 2002 at Westmoreland Hospital. I had my own car again for the whole year. It was a Honda with a sunroof. I could finally get from one place to another and take my children to church again. I started to be happier in my life. Nicholas was still separated from me, and I was still crying over everything that had happened. The hospital called a meeting with everyone present: J. J. L., all the therapists at this time in his life, the doctor, and myself. They were not releasing my son home; this time, they felt it was best for Nicholas to get help through a program. J. J. L. said no, of course; I said yes, get my son the help he needs, the other choice would be foster care placement in the system, and we would never see my son again ever. What choices…none of them were any good, I wanted my son back; God gave my son to me, not anyone else; I was his mother. Get him to help someone done this to him, namely his grandma; I want him strong and living a normal childhood. They came up with a residential program for six months, where he would get the help he needed in Washington, Pennsylvania. So we got to visit very little at first, then we were able to visit more as time went on. The program would work like Nicholas would live a normal life as possible as a child while getting therapy. I know he went fishing a lot; that was peaceful for him, and he also had to do homework. All the staff treated him great there. They were wonderful. After four months, Nicholas had to go to foster care with a therapist for a twenty-four-hour watch to see how he would respond in a house setting. The goal here was to get ready for him to come back home to me. Well, the first placement house did not work out for Nicholas; some fighting had occurred with the other kids in the home. On to the next placement home, they were wonderful, and Nicholas took him to expensive places, but Nicholas had to clean the whole house. Nicholas made friends there in school in New Kensington. Finally, Nicholas was able to come back home to our family. This time I definitely had tears of joy. Nicholas was acting much better. We only stayed one year in Jeanette.

Amen, Amen, Amen

The Youth Services showed up a couple of times; while we lived in Jeanette, D. L. had called them on me. I would tell them the stories about D. L., the ones I knew up to this point. One day after Nicholas came home, we went grocery shopping, then McDonald's for their happy meals for being such good helpers; while grocery shopping, of course, I could only buy small amounts at a time with three little children. For the most part, we tried to have fun in whatever we had to get done. We just pulled in from grocery shopping. I was instructing the children to take one bag of groceries that they could carry along with their happy meal because we had to go up many stairs to get to the top apartment. Once they picked a bag they could carry, they started to go toward the stairs; a maniac came flying down the road real fast and stopped, got out of his car, and his mouth was torn, hanging wide open, staring at the kids and the car. I said, "What now?" He said, "Let's go inside; we need to talk." He even grabbed a couple of bags to help carry them for me. Finally, I heard the words enough is enough; he said, "D. L. called us again; it's clear here: you are a great mother, the kids are being taken care of, I'm closing your case." I said, "Just a minute here; after she did everything to my family and inappropriately touched my sons and their dad, and you're closing the case!" Well, it was unfounded. "Why?" I asked. Well, not enough information.

We believe the older person in a case, and that would be D. L. That the children's Youth Services protect children. What is wrong with this system? Well, he left, and I never had to deal with them again after being harassed ten times. I just wanted justice for everything that happened up to this point; life, sure, was not fair. I wanted J. J. L.'s parents' rights to be taken away forever for the hurt he has caused the children and me for not sticking up for righteousness. Nicholas had to go to a residential program for about eight months; then, he got to come home. The Children Bureau was involved. I believe I talked to about ten different ones. They decided to send him away to get therapy. I believed this helped him, but at the time, this was my little boy. He was under twelve years old. I cried every night. My heart was breaking.

Nicholas continued to act out for the next six years. He had a total of ten admissions at different hospitals.

Then my mom wanted us to come live with them to help me out by babysitting the kids while I worked at my new job and putting K. L. on the school bus for kindergarten. I had to go back to work after being a stay-at-home mom for eight years. While I was at work, I cried a lot over my marriage breaking up, the evilness that happened to my children; a dear co-worker and friend would always give me a hug. Her hugs meant so much to me I knew she cared; it just boosted my spirit up so I could get through my shift.

As I go back in time to September 2003, Nicholas would be nine years old, and Chris would be seven years old, and my daughter would be five years old. I met a really nice man at the hospital while I was working, who came into my life. My friend's name was W. D. He had a wonderful sense of humor that lifted my spirit. I then introduced him to my church and church family. And he gave me hope when I felt hopeless. The first Christmas we spent together, he assembled my children's bicycles; it was a memorable moment. I see the glow on my children's faces as they look at their Christmas presents and the joy that they needed. They were thrilled to get on their bicycles and started to ride them. And found myself looking at my situation differently; I no longer was crying on a daily basis. I was very happy and enjoying my life again. We would take the children to see a movie and out to eat mostly at McDonald's; that is what they enjoyed. Every evening W. D. would spend time talking to the children before they would fall asleep. W. D. helped me more than he would ever know. My children were hurting deeply and were acting out externally. This all made me sad and sick in my stomach. Nicholas was so mean to W. D.; at times, he kicked him, spit on him, and called him names. My situation was terrible. People would judge me; they just did not understand the trauma my family was going through. I know God sent him into my life. I told W. D. about me being in heaven and my vision that God promised me a key whenever I get to the place I'm supposed to be. He asked, "Did you get the key?" I said no, not yet! God said I would get the key! I will get the key. I have faith in God that He will give me the key that He had promised me, and God can not go back on His word. I had introduced W. D. to my church family; he attended Church faithfully. He then was baptized and accepted Jesus Christ as his Lord and Savior.

We stayed for many years with my parents. My friend M. C. from church would stop in to see the children and me. During these times, I had owned a few cars, then I bought a TrailBlazer, which my family loved. We got a lot of use out of it, especially hauling my children and their friends to church, around to and from ball games; it was an extended one, so it would seat eight passengers. We had so much fun in those days. I spent many days on the bleachers watching and enjoying my children playing sports as they were growing up. I remember they made a Leslie House down our street. My children and their friends would go after school a couple of days a week. It was fellowship, games, food, entertainment, and hearing about Jesus. They would have people from our church do the entertainment. It was a blast for the children. Their goal was to have a safe place for children to hang out while their parents worked. One summer, they gave backpacks full of supplies for children to return back to school. It was very helpful.

While we were re-building our lives, everything seemed to be on the right track, and knowing all of this information about my children's grandmother, naturally, I wanted to protect my daughter K. L., so the same thing wouldn't happen to her that happened to my boys.

Whenever K. L. was eight years old, well, another bomb just went off in my house despite all of my efforts of trying to protect my daughter. With J. J. L. having custody, one day K. L. told me her story about what her grandmother had done to her. I was devastated, and I felt that all of my efforts to protect her had failed. Respecting my daughter's wishes, I will not be writing about her story. With the effort of her counselor, I was able to call the Children and Youth Services. The Children and Youth Services instructed me to call the police. I asked the police, "What are you going to do?" The chief of police said, "We have a conflict of interest, and I am going to turn it over to the DA's office." The DA contacted me; we set up an appointment for him to talk to me. I went into the office for an appointment to talk to Marcus, the DA; I took a lie detector test and passed with flying colors. He said, "You don't have anything to worry about—you passed." Then he proceeded to tell me that J. J. L., his mom, and dad refused to take a lie detector test. Well, you can see what's going on here: who then lied about the whole story and who was telling the truth. Previously, I had J. J. L.'s, Nicholas's, and Chris's story, and now I have K. L.'s story. I have been fighting for custody, trying to get the kids from J. J. L. because he was defending his mother, and I thought, as a parent, it would be better for the children not to be around their grandmother for what she had done. Well, this had to be proven in court before this could happen. My children would not tell anyone else but me about their story. This was not good enough to prove this case. They loved their father regardless of how he was as a person, and they loved getting money and gifts from their grandparents. This seemed to be what was important to them at the time. They were children. All this evilness this one woman caused to my family, my broken home, and brought shame, humiliation to my children. This did not matter to my children; they were so deeply hurt that nothing mattered to them. They were just not talking to anyone about all their hurt. Nicholas did talk at his last admission at Monsour Hospital. Then he became very violent, acting out, so he had to be sent away for therapy. He was sent to a residential facility in Washington, Pennsylvania. Nicholas was about nine years old. The whole process took about eight months. This seemed like an eternity. After eight months, Nicholas was able to come home, but he still had to do therapy. He started the wrap-around service. He had many counselors who worked wonderfully with him; thanks to all their effort and hard work, Nicholas turned his life around. Although he claimed nothing ever happened to him, he had to have therapy until he was twelve years old. He quit taking his medicine, and he did not need therapy anymore.

In the summer of 2008, although I have had wonderful experiences that happen in my life, Christopher, when he was twelve years old, decided to hit a basketball with a baseball bat. The ball and the bat came backward and smacked him right in the mouth. I picked him up from his friend's house; there was blood everywhere. We went straight to the hospital to find out he had to get sutures in his lip. Apparently, he bit his lip open, also broke half of his front right tooth off. I could just imagine how much pain my poor son had to be going through. Christopher went to the dentist and had to see a couple of specialists. Eventually, Christopher received his fake youth tooth. Needless to say, I spent the next few years making payments for his tooth, it was a struggle but a blessing having his tooth replaced.

Rebuilding My Life

My life was changing for the better: Nicholas was baptized when he was sixteen years old. My other two children were baptized prior to years before Nicholas was baptized.

At this point in time, when I'm writing this book, Nicholas is twenty-two years old and doing great. He was in the Marines for a couple of years, and now he is going to college for business and living his dream of playing football for a semi-pro team. I give all the glory to God for helping him through all of this stuff he endured in his younger years. I always made sure my kids went to church as they were growing up. They all three were baptized. Chris is now twenty years old, and he is currently in the Marine Corps station in California. K. L. is seventeen years old. I'm still working on her coming back to church. God promises me this would happen, and His word would not come back void. My children will serve and be faithful to the Lord. I am trusting God for His promises in my children's life. Christopher quit going to outpatient therapy when he was fourteen. Christopher faithfully attended church with me, his mother, at the Word of Life Ministries in Greensburg, Pennsylvania, until he left for the Marines.

People Who Inspired Me after Going Through Trauma from My First Marriage and the Divorce

I was hurting so much I felt numb to everyone around

me. I decided this one day to sign up for a woman's mentoring ministry connecting heart to heart at my church, The Word of Life Ministries. I met C. F., who I was matched up with to be my mentor. She would write me a love letter once a month to encourage me. I found three of her love letters starting in September 2007 and ending in November 2007. And I must say this was just what I needed, what I was going through in my life at this time. One scripture that she wrote in one of her letters was Hebrews 12: 15 (KJV), "Looking diligently lest any man fail of the grace of God; lest any root of bitterness springing up trouble you, and thereby many be defiled." This helped me; I surely did not want to plant any seeds of bitterness in my life. We would talk on the telephone a few times, we went to the mentoring luncheon together at the church, and we also had lunch with tea in Scottdale, at Miss Maratha's Tea room. Also, we would talk a lot at church whenever we would see each other. This, I must say, was the far best encouragement that I could ever receive, and I had gained a true friend through this process. Today we are still friends. I see her very little at church.

One day after church, I gave C. F. and her husband a ride home, and oh, what a blessing that was to have them and Janet G. in my car at the same time. I just felt so loved around all of them. I had met Janet G. at the Word of Life;

oh, what a blessing to know her. We had become friends, and still today, I give her rides to and from church. I had found a love letter from Janet G. written ten years ago; oh, how she encouraged me…what a blessing to have her in my life. Both of them—dear heart sisters in Christ; great women of faith have connected with my heart, and therefore I have become a woman of great faith. I appreciate all the love that they have shown me over the years and still are going on.

Another dear friend of mine is Charlotte Dunn, who I had met a few years ago at church. She has shown me so much love, faith, and always helping people by doing all that she can to help people out. After church Sunday, I went to visit Charlotte, who is a widow and in her eighties. I had extra leftover stuff green peppers that I made, so I brought them with me to Charlotte's house. She was so appreciative of her dinner. I found out that she did not have plans of making herself anything to eat. I felt blessed that I was able to bless her with dinner. She would always cook for her husband and for the whole neighborhood. She has a good heart and much love to give. I am so blessed to have these three wonderful sisters in my life today. I feel like we are all family at the Word of Life.

Another dear sister in Christ I met at the Word of Life Ministries—E. T. This one day, I decided to sit at her table along with A. S. at ladies' Bible study group. I enjoyed meeting older women to encourage me and learn knowledge from them. Two weeks later, I sat at their table again, this time E. T. shared with me something very special. E. T. was shopping at Oldies, and God spoke to her. E. T. heard from God; then she was obedient and acted on what God told her to do. She did it. It was to buy me this very special gift, a brass box with a key attached to the front of it holding scripture cards in it. E. T. did not know what this meant, but I sure did. This is what God said to me whenever I was up in His house, whenever I was fourteen years old, "Whenever you get to the place I want you to be, I will give you the key." My friends, this is exactly what took place years later, in 2007. God was faithful in His words. God loves us all; we can trust Him. God will never let you down; just learn to obey Him.

C. F., my mentor at this time, wrote to me in a letter on September 5, 2007, stating that event about E. T. gave me the scripture box with the key because the scriptures have all the answers that we seek and the comfort in them for us to relax in His arms while the Lord works everything out for us. We just have to have faith and keep growing in understanding and knowledge of His Word until we learn that, which is unending. C. F., you nailed it. I could not have said that any better; you are awesome! That is so true, which I have found out over the years since receiving my letter from C. F. and my gift from God through E. T. Whenever you're obedient to Him, He will ask more of us, and your life will get much better. This is so God's will be done in your life, not your will, and much will be accomplished for His kingdom. I remember driving down the road, I was hearing from God to pull over and pick up cans from the side of the road. That is exactly what I did. This taught me to be humble in my life. My relationship with God grew stronger, and my faith was growing too. It seems like I am going up levels in my life and falling deeper in love with God. I give God all the honor, praise, glory, and love forever and ever; Amen, Amen, and Amen!

LIVING MY LIFE

In 2008 while I was working at Excela Health hospital in Greensburg, Pennsylvania, my boss asked us, employees, "Who would like to work over at Jeanette Hospital?" I heard God's voice say, "I want you to go," so I went. In 2010, near the end of my time working there, I was placed in the Intensive Care Unit. One day, I went into a room where something started happening. I was getting goosebumps, those funny-looking bumps whenever your hair stands up on your arms, and it's a good feeling you have inside of you.

Amen, Amen, Amen

I remembered Brian had a severe car accident, and since he lived in Jeannette, he would have been brought to this ICU. While standing next to the empty bed, I decided to immediately look up to reminisce that I was standing there with God looking down at Brian when he had died in his accident in 2003. He would have seen me with God. However, I was standing here with God looking down at Brian in the year 1981; I was fourteen years old when he showed me my future and Brian as a man in 2003. At this point in my life, I had not talked to Brian for years since we had met in person in 2001. I didn't know Brian when I was fourteen years old. When God showed me my future Brian as a dead man, then God brought him back to life again.

My friend M. C. and I are talking about her teaching me to ride a motorbike. One day, M. C. decided I needed to live outside my box to do something adventurous. I agreed with her, and soon I went to buy a motorbike with M. C.'s help. Of course, she had to ride it home for me. I knew absolutely nothing about riding a motorbike that was definitely living outside my box. M. C. would come over, take me down to East Park, and taught me how to ride my bike and shift the gears. I then took a class at Westmoreland county community college to learn to ride my motorbike safely. It did not take me long before I learned to ride comfortably. M. C. said that

Rebuilding My Life

I was a fast learner. Then I started to ride my children around on my motorbike. I didn't want them to be fearful of trying new things and being fearful of things in life like their dad. I would ride Nicholas on the back whenever we delivered newspapers. One time, I went up this huge hill; whenever we got to the top, Nicholas said, "Mom, you did a wheelie." He was not impressed at all. I would have to say he was a little fearful. One summer, Nicholas has summer school. I would pick him up after school with the motorbike; needless to say, he would be quite embarrassed to ride in front of his friends. Near the end of summer school, he started to like riding the motorbike with me. Christopher was fearful just riding in general, but he would go with me up to Ohiopyle and back. We would get ice cream cones on the way back home. Christopher just loved it. K. L. loved riding with me. She went everywhere with me on the motorbike. We would ride up to Ohiopyle and back; she could not get enough riding in, just absolutely loved it. I would ride my motorbike to work and back; it saved me in gas money. Whenever I would ride my motorbike, I felt like I had accomplished something in my life. It felt like I was truly free. Another joyful memory is when my son Nicholas at the age of sixteen, along with his friend B. H., was baptized at our church. At this time, he was more settled down in his life.

Amen, Amen, Amen

Finally, I paid around one thousand dollars to move out on our own in Greensburg and rented half a duplex in the year 2012; I loved it there. My friend M. C. from the Word of Life owned the house. M. C. was a rock for me the whole time we have been friends.

One day in June 2012, Brian and I were married. Things were different this time, around the total opposite of how my life was with Brian in 2001. Remember I told you how he helped me back then. Well, it wasn't long I found out he was an alcoholic. He now had a plate in his head from his bad car crash in 2003, where he died, and God brought him back to life. It had been confirmed from Brian's ex-wife Dawn, who was with him on that day by his side holding his hand. One day at the hospital while I was working, Dawn, who was a patient at the time, told me how the doctors told her he died. Then not long, the doctors told her he was alive. Dawn explained to me that God brought him back to life. Well, Brian was a completely different person in 2012. He drank himself into confusion and was definitely very verbally abusive toward me. He stole a credit card and put all the blame on me legally. One time, he drove drunk and was very reckless. He stated, "If I didn't love you, I would throw you out of my truck." While the truck was moving, he stated this to me. I started praying to God that he would get me out of this situation alive. I was fearful at this point; I didn't know what would happen next. Shortly after this, Brian wanted to know why I married him. I said, "God wanted me to do something in your life, but I don't know what it is." We were driving on a little road trip that ended up coming back home in a few hours. Brian proceeds to tell me about seeing me with God after he wrecked. I said, "I know I was with God when I was fourteen years old." God showed me my future, and you were dead with tubes coming out from your body, and you were a man. I told Brian I had his letter he sent me in 2004 about this. I said to God, "This man is dead!" God replies, "Not for long, I want you to blah, blah, something in his life." God never told me what I was to do in Brian's life. We got back home from our little road trip. Brian did some bad things like stolen and wrecked my brand new white Malibu after we separated, waiting for our divorce. He racked up three credit cards in my name and maxed them out. Stole my rewards card from Giant Eagle, cashed a bunch of bad checks in my name. He made up lies and put a total of three PFAs against me. After eight months, our divorce was final. I was so happy to get out of that situation. I still was trying to figure out what I was to do in his life. It was such a mess, and Brian thinks that he just made my life a mess. We still lived in separate places while we were married.

Needless to say, it took me five years to straighten up my finances that had been destroyed in eight months. So I didn't talk to Brian for many years after that.

While still living in our duplex, one day, some kids broke into our house, kicked the basement door opened while I was there alone. The kids were at their dad's on visitation. I called 911 and watched through the peephole. I could see flip-flops, and it sounded like the neighbor kids. They started up two basement steps, a locked door between us; I quickly changed my voice in the deepest voice I could and said, "Who's there?" They quickly ran out the basement door the way they came in. It took the police forever to arrive. I called the kids because they were due home. K. L. called my mom and said, "We are moving back in with you." I said, "No, we are not." I just got comfortable living on my own. So I took the telephone from K. L., and my mom said, "Please come and live with us." I said, "We just moved out. Okay, if I move back, I'm not moving out again; I'm there to stay, I'm tired of moving back and forth, and it cost too much money." My daughter, K. L., and I moved back in with my parents, and my two sons moved in with their dad. They did not want to move back in with my parents.

April 20, 2017, I bought my dad and mom's house. This was my dad's wish that my mom would have a place to live if something would ever happen to him watching his younger brothers pass away one by one.

In 2019, my dad became ill with kidney failure and started dialysis three times a week. My sister and I would make arrangements with each other to drop off and pick my dad up from dialysis. This was a very hard journey in watching my dad's health decline rapidly. My dad and I would watch TV and talk for hours. Then he wanted to go fishing; near the end of his life, he made three fishing days. He had a blast and caught a fish. We made his fishing days a big family event. My dad had a final request to go see 9/11 up in Shanksville, Pennsylvania, with all his sisters and anyone else that could make it. That is exactly what happened; we all went up as a group. On September 22, 2019, I lost my best friend, my dad. I miss him so dearly. My dad will never know the outcome of my situation, what I went through for years waiting for justice to be done. He will never get to see or read my book that I am now writing. Although my dad lived to be eighty years old, he outlived all his younger brothers, who all passed away in their seventies; life is just too short.

IN THE PRESENT TIME

One day at work in January 2020, I was bringing up a linen cart with a co-worker from the basement to the first floor. This was not my job, but it needed to be done. Whenever we were getting off the elevator on the first floor, low and beheld, Brian was holding the elevator doors for us. Now I want you to know before this time; I have not spoken to Brian in years. He started to talk to me. I was feeling a little uneasy. On September 14, 2019, I was on a ventilator, my daughter was going to pull the plug, and my sister said no; then I came out of it and off the ventilator. It was a near-death experience for him. I didn't say much to him. I quickly told him about my situation with my dad taking him to dialysis three days a week. My sister and I would make arrangements to take and pick him up for his treatments. Then I went on to say we lost him on September 22, 2019, and he was my best friend that I ever had. We left. And I got back to work, and that was the last time I talked to Brian. Although I thought that would be the very last time I would ever talk to Brian, we were finished. Oh no, I have more to talk about. Later on, I found myself praying to God about forgiving me for unforgiving I might have had against Brian whenever I thought I had forgiven him for all the damage and hurt he caused in my life. I was asking for forgiveness and forgiving all the people in my past that I could think of and forgiving people unconsciously that I was not thinking of; I wanted to be in the right standing with God. After all, he wanted me to do something in his life, and I still not sure what it is exactly. I started to feel free in my life and much peace that I didn't have before.

On February 4, 2020, a patient coughed in my face as I was leaving their room; I felt the germ go back in my throat, I was thinking I'm going to get sick. I started to pray I would not get this virus that everyone started to talk about. I could not afford to get sick. I'm single, own my own home and rely on my mother, who lives with me, to pay the utility bills so we can make it. We were in a bind after my father passed. However, I'm getting the mess straightened out. Everything is starting to look up in my life. I am starting to fix up the place getting new siding put on soon. I just got a new roof put on two years ago. Well, I worked for two weeks. I started to cough and have some mucus. I felt great. I went to my friend's house, who I would stay for six hours, and care for their dad to give them a break. My friend said, "Are you sick?" I said no, I wasn't; I had a little cough but felt fine. I said, "I'm going to wear a mask to keep him safe." That was my last day there, not knowing what was about to happen.

Sunday, on February 23, 2020, I started to become short of breath; my respiration was rapid, so I went to Frick Hospital to the emergency room. The doctor and nurse asked me a lot of questions, and I answered them. The conversation went like this: a patient coughed in my face on February 4, 2020, I looked on their chart, and there I saw coronavirus was written; I didn't have any idea what that meant. The doctor basically said that would not have been on there; it just came out. In China, they had an outbreak in December, which means the virus was there before December; that is common sense. One other thing that happened that no one mentioned at all was on January 5, 2020: a bus wrecked on our turnpike, no one could speak English, and they were coming from New York. There were some Chinese people on that bus. This came from a source that knew about the wreck. So they gave me medicine and sent me home. The next day I was a little worse; I then went down to Allegheny General to get a second opinion. They did another chest X-ray, they said, "It showed bronchitis." I had bronchitis before; it was nowhere near this bad. Gave me more medicine and sent me home. I made a follow-up appointment with my PCP. On the day of the appointment, which was that Wednesday, I arrived at the doctor's office and had a hard time breathing; very short of breath. My doctor told them to tell me to go to the emergency room. So I went back down to Allegheny General Hospital. The doctors ordered breathing treatments for me, highly recommended tea with honey and gave me more medicines, and sent me home. Friday, I had my first doctor's visit. She ordered me a nebulizer for home and allergy medicine. I never had an allergy like this in my life. It was too late to buy the nebulizer after my doctor's appointment. I made it through the weekend. On Monday, March 02, 2020, I went back to Frick's emergency room. I was very short of breath. I told them I needed a breathing treatment and a nebulizer for home. They hooked me up. I finally had everything I needed to take care of myself at home. My doctor ordered that I see a pulmonary doctor, so I did. He started to test me for everything, including a respiratory panel. The Health Department was only testing if you meet the criteria; I was not, so I did not get tested for COVID-19. My doctor ordered me to see a cardiac doctor, everything normal for my age there. All my tests were normal. I had another doctor's appointment on March 13. My PCP decided to test me for COVID-19; they were allowing anyone to get tested at this point. Well, my test was negative for COVID-19. I was happy and thanking God I was healthy and well. I still had rapid respiration, which means I was fighting off a virus, just not the COVID-19. I was out of work from February 21, 2020, to April 12, 2020. During this time, I was not doing much: I would pray a lot, read God's Word, and post scriptures on Facebook. My faith was tempted, but I kept my faith by the end of this trial. I had greater faith than when it all started. While I was at home, I had a dream that was so real on March 05, 2020. To my left were dark staircase steps leading down; straight in front of me, I see a lit-up staircase going down, a dark-haired lady in a white robe standing against a brown wall, standing still and saying, "The truth will come out." Then at the exact same time, while she was saying this, a beige-covered wagon went down; this lit up the staircase and back up again and stopped in front of the lady, standing against the wall. Then the second time the wagon went down, this lit up the staircase; a lady's voice coming from inside the wagon, which you couldn't see, was saying, "I just want to know the truth." Then back to the lady, standing against the brown wall, said, "Something happened a long time ago; the truth will come out." I asked the lady against the brown wall. As the wagon went down the stairs, I could see her, "Is this the way to the ER?" I pointed to my left. "No! You don't want to go that way; you want to go that way," pointing to my right, she said. I made a right and ended up on the street walking to Westmoreland. I thought of the hospital, but I could see the mall ahead of me. Just then, my sister popped in beside me; I said, "Good, you're here; you can give me a ride to the hospital." My sister answered me and said, "I did not bring the car; I walked." That means we have to walk the rest of the way and back again; you don't have a vehicle here. Then

Rebuilding My Life

I was in another place saying, "I've never been here before."
I woke up as I was opening the door to an ER. The next
day I went to Dr. Lee's office, my pulmonary specialist, at
Canonsburg Hospital. This was my first time ever here. His
office door was right by the emergency room entrance door
to the hospital. What happened a long time ago, the truth will
come out; wow, that would be my situation. Whenever the
children were little, we never had justice or our day in court.
We are still waiting for all the truth to come out. *Wow!* God
was moving in my life. While I was off work, I would listen
to Joyce Myers CDs. After listening to her CDs, my spirits
were lifted up. One of her CDs was a lesson on faith and
fear. I really was empowered with faith after listening to her
speak. I just love her and how she tells it like it is. I would
listen to her on the television program she comes on; I just
love it! I'm waiting for the opportunity to see her in person
and hear her speak live in concert. Joyce reminds us to ask
God to reveal Himself to us, ask for whatever we want, pray
bold prayers, ask big or for a lot instead of too little, pray
for His power, His wisdom, His goodness, and pray for an
increase in understanding. Remember that Jesus wins in the
end; the book of Revelations tells us so. The first post I made
on March 7, on Facebook, was telling each of my adult children that I loved them very much, their mother forever. I felt

the worst I had ever felt in my life. I did not know if I was going to wake up the next day. I was very short of breath and had trouble breathing. My air shut off at one point; I started to motion for my mother, I could not breathe; I was sitting on the couch, my feet dangle on the floor, just then I heard the Lord's voice say, "Put your head down as low as you can between your legs and cough as hard as you can." I did just that; it was a hard loud cough, and up came a very small amount of mucus. I could breathe again! I started thanking Jesus for helping me, started praising God, and giving God all the glory! Amen, Amen, and Amen! Hallelujah! I knew in my heart everything would be all right, and I would wake up tomorrow. In the second post I made on March 13, on Facebook, I was thanking everyone for their prayers, waiting on test results; I thank God every day that I woke up, and I wanted everyone to have a blessed day. The third post I made was on March 14 about C.O.V.I.D.=19, Christ, Over, Infection, Diseases Joshua 1:9; I copied that from a Facebook post, then I added to that the scripture Psalm 91:3-4, which I found very helpful for what I was going through at this time in my life.

> Surely He shall deliver you from the snare of the fowler and from the perilous pestilence. He shall cover you with

Rebuilding My Life

His feathers, and under His wings you shall take refuge; His truth shall be your shield and buckler.

Psalm 91:3-4

The fourth post I made was on March 16: C.O.V.I.D.=19 (Christ, Over, Victory, In, Deliver). I made this one up because of what I was going through; this scripture seemed to help me, the most Psalm 91. God protects and defends us. The fifth post I made was on March 19, test results in—I am negative for coronavirus! Yes! I still need your prayers; I have a virus. I'm very short of breath and cough but no fever. Thank you all for your prayers, I love all of you, and you're in my prayers. The sixth post I made on March 22, on Facebook, asking everyone to ride out the storm with great faith, Jesus lives in us, by God's grace. This, too, will pass away! It's all God's power! After all, Peter walked on water! In the seventh post I also made on March 22, on Facebook, there was an invitation for people to accept Jesus Christ as their personal Lord and Savior. This was stepping out of my comfort zone; I was empowered by this journey whenever I was home sick with some virus. In the eighth post I made on March 24, on Facebook, just giving an update that I had with my pulmonary doctor by telephone appointment; I still had symptoms from this virus I had. I was still coughing and had rapid respiration. He believed this would not harm me and followed up with my PCP on April 3. I am healed. Praise God! Thank you, Lord Jesus! Thank you for all your prayers. What I was learning to do was live in faith, by faith, and Jesus is Lord of the coronavirus. On March 25, 2020, you were not going to believe this, but I was actually enjoying my journey that I was on. My prayer would be that God's will be done in my life, not my own will, and the journey I was on would be from God. I was asking, "Lord, show me, guide me, love me, Lord, and love you, Lord." I was also saying, "Protect me, defend me, and fight for me, Lord." I realized I needed to show forgiveness when my co-workers came against me for stupid reasons and no gossiping about others. Romans 12:10, "Be kindly affectionate to one another with brotherly love, in honor giving preference to one another." This was reminding me of what I needed to change in my life. These things need to be done: girdle your tongue, love my co-workers, trust in their love for me, do not question others about what they were doing when they meant to harm me. It does not matter. I am a child of God; I am attending Word of Life, I am going to worship God with all my heart, every service focuses on only God, I will block everyone and everything out of my mind. I love my Lord, my God with all my heart, soul, mind, and might. Nothing is going to harm me; what was meant to harm me, God will turn into good! We will get through this together. Also, I was reminded to write this book and stop procrastinating. That was a sure change. I'm writing my book as we speak. The ninth post I made on March 26, on Facebook, I had a test done for my oxygen yesterday, on March 25; it was normal, but I still had symptoms like respiration kicked up to over one hundred beats per minute, became fatigued, and needed a break. Then four hours later, after the test, I was at home sitting on my couch resting. My sister counted my respiration. They were thirty-eight per minute, which were still rapid, but I'm moving right along. Then at the end of that same post in 2 Timothy 1:7, "For God has not given us a spirit of fear, but of power and of love and of a sound mind." Through the Holy Spirit, I will overcome these symptoms, and they too shall pass! I am healthy and well! I was believing by faith, trusting in God, and I am healed. Also, on this day, I was reminded to "be still and know that I am God." While on my journey at home, I would pray for forgiveness toward anyone I had not forgiven yet at this point in my life. I was asking for forgiveness and forgiving all the people in my past that I could think of and forgiving people unconsciously that I was not thinking of; I just wanted to be in the right standing with God. Anyone that came to my mind, I would ask for forgiveness for that person. Whenever Brian came to mind, I asked God if I truly forgave him for everything he put me through. And I wanted to know If I accomplished whatever I was to do in his life; after all, he wanted me to do something in his life, and I am still not sure what it is exactly. I started to feel free in my life and much peace that I didn't have before. I started to question my life about what I was doing before I got sick, and here a person that I forgave from church kissed her husband in front of me with this attitude to make me jealous. I questioned why she acted like that; it was her husband, not mine. That is what husbands and wives do. You see, that evil spirit came into my thoughts for that moment in time, and I spent the next five weeks battling this in my life along with this virus. I learned not to question people's attitudes; it just is not worth it. You see, I brought this friend to my church, and he married this other person at my church. They do have my blessing that their marriage will work. I am over that whole situation. I give God all the praise and all the glory in Jesus' name; Amen, Amen, and Amen. Then on April 5, 2020, this scripture came to me; it was on my mind. Matthew 6:33 (KJV), "But seek ye first the kingdom of God, and his righteousness; and all these things shall be added unto you." Whenever I was pondering upon this scripture, I realized how important it was to do. This includes everything in my life going to my Father in prayer first before I act on a decision. Go to church first to worship God before doing anything else in my life. My journey was ending at home. I must return to work, and bills were not going to pay themselves.

On April 12, 2020, I was able to return to work with a sit-down job, watching heart monitors for two weeks; this is all I did. I still had a few symptoms. I must say much better. I was on my way to a full recovery. It was a great feeling to be back at work to see my co-workers when not too long ago, I was not sure if I was going to wake up again. I appreciated my life more again, thanking God for my job and my co-workers. I can actually say I truly missed everyone. One of my co-workers came up to me and said, "Good to see you back, and your ex-husband was on our floor while you were gone." I said, "Really? He is usually not on our floor, and thanks for telling me." Thoughts came rushing through my mind at that moment about Brian just wondering about him. It was January this year when I had seen him last and when he was holding the elevator door open for my coworker and me. He was already discharged yesterday, so I did not see him. My co-workers throughout the day came up to me and were happy to see I was back at work with them. We have a few new staff members that joined our team, and sad to learn, a lot of our nurses that were friends had left our team whenever COVID-19 hit our hospital. I wanted to add not a hard hit. The numbers stayed low. I was impressed with all the changes that took place. It was a different environment than when I left ill six weeks ago and came back to a different new world. The saying I was hearing was we would get through this together. I knew this is where I need to be in a time such as this.

By the end of this week, April 18, Brian was on our floor as a patient. My boss wanted to know if this was a problem that Brian was on our floor, and I told her no. I was working the monitors whenever he came out of his room and saw me for the first time since January. He looked at the board to see my name, then looked at me with a mask on it; hard to tell who anyone is these days, he said, "I was married to a Donna once." I waved to him to say that it was me. He couldn't believe that it was me. Immediately, he came over to me then started talking, trying to catch up with lost times, but he was sick and needed a few new organs. Finally, the nurse was getting mad, so he went back to his room. After my shift, I went home. I was doing a lot of praying about what I am supposed to do in his life. Now that he is back at the hospital on my floor, where I work, I won't be getting out of this one, but I would never want to. I am obedient to God's will; wherever He leads me, I'll follow Him. I am trying to get answers here about what I am supposed to do. All I got at this point was peace about the situation. It's like you know something is going to take place. You just want to know beforehand, but sometimes you just live through it and do the best you can and pray for the Lord's guidance to see you through it to the other side. While you go through it, Jesus is with you; He will never leave or forsake you.

The next day I return to work for my shift, I brought with me a book to give to Brian to read. I just finished reading it while I was down; it was about illness due to not forgiving it was a spiritual thing to overcome. It helped me in my life to see things in life that I was overlooking that needed to be dealt with. Perhaps, Brian is one thing that follows me that needs to be dealt with. I also gave Brian a copy of this book what I have written so far up to this point, the part where he did see me with God. We talked throughout my shift, then I left. The next day I brought with me the letter that he wrote me in 2003, a very important letter that he track me down to give to me. I gave it to Brian to read while I was working. Then after my shift, I went to his room to talk. I was not sure how this was going to go, but here it goes. Brian said he didn't have his glasses to read this letter, so I offered to read it to him. That is what I did—read the letter to him. He immediately apologized for everything he put me through while we were married. I told him I forgave him and said If there was anything I did to please forgive me. He said it was him, and I didn't do anything wrong to him. We only talked for a short while; then I left to go home; I was tired at this point. The very next day, I went to work; Brian was discharged and gone. I felt good about what took place; I had peace with the situation.

Today on June 27, 2020, I had a major breakthrough in my life. What I was praying for in the year 2000, the truth came out, and my son Nicholas finally opened up to me and told his side of the story when he was from ages five to eight. We talked for hours about our situation, and I cried when I was telling him what I remembered that happened to him and our family. Nicholas is presently twenty-six years old. It has been confirmed—our mother and son bond has been strengthened that was once broken at a young age due to evilness.

Whenever Brian was admitted on other floors, he came down to talk to me. He started to invite me up to his room to talk. I only could stay for short visits. I had to get home to my mother, who I needed to help take care of; just a little help, she needed not much. Basically, she needs someone there; at night, she gets lonely while I work and out of the house for eight hours. Since I got back to work, I have seen Brian many times at the hospital; we became friends. We would walk outside around the hospital and make small talk remembering the good memories. I would bring him food: he wanted tomato soup and grilled cheese, and two other times I made him Chicken Parmesan. Then his appetite started to decrease, and he started requesting chocolate milk for a while. In June 2020, we would talk about forgiveness and forgiving; so God could forgive him, and I asked if he has been making a menace with people he hurt according to this important letter that he wrote in 2003, and he replied, "Pretty much so." On this one day, I gave him a copy of this letter, took it to his room, and put it on his bag, where he could see it. The letter is when he was truly a changed man. I talked to him on the cell phone; he was out for testing. Then Brian became too weak to walk. I would push him in his wheelchair outside just a short distance only a few times. Apparently, the staff would see him out and about in his wheelchair; they would help him out. Whenever Brian was getting weaker physically, he started to struggle to stay alive. At the beginning of July, Brian ended back up in the ICU. My friend Linda, who is also a sister in Christ, attends my church; also, works at the same hospital that I do. She walked into Brian's room, found him struggling, immediately started to shake him, call his name, and they had to call a code. On July 7, I talked to Brian on my cell phone, and he told me to cancel all his requests as he was being moved to another floor. I arrived at the hospital for my shift, and his door was closed. They told me some bad news. I opened his door and peeked as he was in a deep sleep, so I closed his door. Later that same day, he woke up. I handed him a dinner tray, said, "Goodbye, Brian." They escorted him up to a different floor in the hospital, not knowing that would be my last time I would physically see Brian and the last time to hear his voice on my cell phone. On Friday, July 10, Brian texted me that he was at a different hospital; he was bad, and in so much pain that we will talk later; he was going to lay down and take a nap. Well, that never happened; we did not get to talk later. I tried to call him and text him, but no answer. On July 16, I received a text from his sister telling me Brian was going. I was working and didn't get to read the text until two hours later. I text back to say I might not make it; I was working. Then It was too late; he already passed on two hours ago. I just wanted to pray for his mother and family. Brian was always concerned about his mother's well-being. In one of the conversations we had, Brian said, "My poor mother!" Then eight days later, his mother also passed away.

It was our first day back to church on a Wednesday night

Rebuilding My Life

service on August 5, 2020, since the COVID-19 happened. I was glad to be there, but I believe I'm leaving soon. I believe I got a word from God at church from Pastor Tom. The word went something like this: put your past behind you and move into your future. I prayed to God before this about a word; it was that whole week about this very thing. I said, "Lord, you give me confirmation through someone I can trust like Pastor Tom, then I know that I'm leaving this church." That is exactly what happened. I'm leaving this church. I just don't know when or where I'm going yet. When the time comes, I'll know exactly what to say or do. Jesus is with me everywhere I go; where he leads me, I'll follow *Him*. The scripture is Philippians 3:13 (KJV), but I don't want to leave out also verse 14, which is the ultimate goal, "Brethren, I count not myself to have apprehended: but this one thing that I do forgetting those things which are behind, and reaching forth unto those things which are before, I press toward the mark for the prize of the high calling of God in Christ Jesus." Maybe within a year, I will be leaving; not sure when. I won't leave until the plan is complete and I know where I'm going next. This month I have been there nineteen years since Brian brought me to this church. Also, this is what God said would happen, and it sure did. God said, "I will lead you to a place that doesn't exist, but it will, through a friend."

Amen, Amen, Amen

Thank you, Lord, for your faithfulness in my life! The Lord will fulfill His purpose for me in my life. Psalm 138:8, "The Lord will perfect that which concerns me; Your mercy, O Lord, endures forever; Do not forsake the works of Your hands." How awesome is that! I give you all the glory and honor, *Amen, Amen, and Amen!*

On September 9, 2020, my friend Janet G. called for a ride to church, so I picked her. Then she handed me a journal book to write in, and on the outside cover, it reads: "For I know the plans I have for you," declares Lord in Jeremiah 29:11. I felt so special to be blessed with a gift and to have such a special friend as Janet. I have been picking her up for church for a while now. This reminds me of how my friend from my old church, L. B., would pick me up all the time for church whenever I was just fourteen years old; also, that is when I had my encounter with God. If it wasn't for Laura taking me to church being faithful in doing so, I might not have the faith that I have today, and for her, I am forever thankful. I appreciated all the rides to church and all that she has done for me. I feel blessed that I am able to give Janet rides to church just like Laura has done for me in the past. The scripture on the front cover of my journal book fits my life perfectly. God is moving in my life, and I know the plans are coming about; my life is changing financially, it's getting the flow of money that is becoming free.

My mom told me she was moving out, which means I'm going to be left standing in my house. My mom has been dependent almost her whole life; depending on my dad and that he has been gone one year now, she wants her independence. She is seventy-nine years old and needs to be supervised for when she passes out and falls. Also, she doesn't understand a lot about life, things like paying bills. I need to help her, and now she doesn't want my help. This is causing a whole lot of stress for me. I realized after my mom was moving out that my love language is doing for other people; this makes me feel loved. I started to feel like my world was spinning out of control. Then I started to pray about my situation for the right answer in making decisions on what I was going to do. I bought my parents' house for my mom. It was my dad's wish, so my mom would have a place to live, and I would have some shelter. So I had to arrange my finances so I could buy the house. I took out a loan to combine the bills that I already had. I had paid most of my bills off. I put a new roof on the house. Of course, I paid someone to do that for me. I fixed up the bathtub and shower, went through a company by the name of West Home Shores, and that bill will be paid off this coming March. If my mom moves out, I won't have enough money to pay the utilities. However, next year will be better for me financially; then, I will be able to afford the utilities. I will have to re-organize my finances. I just need to make the right decisions. For example, I need the internet to write my book. I think the devil is mad because I have been writing my book after procrastinating for many years. Well, I've been down and keeping the faith that everything will work out. I texted a friend and asked for some laughs to be sent my way, and he sent me some ha and hees; well, it worked, I started to laugh; it wasn't long I felt much better. I knew I could count on my friend Robert to make me laugh, just like when we were teenagers. Well, it only took three days to get some great news. My mom told me she had a dream last night with my dad, and he told her not to move out. She woke up happy and singing. The great news is, she is staying and not moving out. The stress is all gone. The good that came out from all of this I found cheaper car insurance, and we got a discount on our monthly cable bill. The best part was sharing a special moment with a friend through a text. It has been a long time since we had shared a special moment together; it was back when we were teenagers. I will continue to work on writing my book, and someday soon, I hope to have it completed.

I'm presently fifty-four years old, and I have not had the opportunity to see the B. family. Whenever I said goodbye,

Rebuilding My Life

I was twenty-one years old, after my vacation was over in Texas, and Robert drove me to the airport.

On Wednesday, October 7, 2020, my church, the one I attend for services, closed down for services on Wednesday night again, the second close down of Wednesday night services since COVID-19 hit us. There were a couple of cases of COVID in the church this time around. This saddens my heart. I'm always looking forward to Wednesday night services which strengthen my faith to get through the rest of the week until Sunday morning services. Then I got a phone call. I was exposed to COVID-19 by a patient who passed away and was positive. I'm doing fine. I just want all of this COVID to go away forever.

On October 24, 2020, I had my training gear up to go into COVID rooms. I will be taking care of COVID-19 patients on my floor at work until this is all over.

Since November 2020, I have been going into COVID-19 patients' rooms. I perform my duties as a technical partner, which is similar to a nurse's aide but more on-the-job training skills. I am also a technical partner two; I watch the heart monitors on the units that have them. Whenever I am in a COVID room, I try to talk to them and spend a few extra minutes with them; so I'm not running out of the room. I try to get close to look them in the eyes whenever I'm talking to them, touch their arm and hold their hands for a few minutes. I want them to know I'm here for them so they won't be afraid. I want them to feel special too. If they ask me to pray for them, I say a prayer for them in the room before I leave them.

On Wednesday, December 23, 2020, my church, the one I attend for services, opened back up for services on Wednesday nights again. I am so happy to be attending church again on Wednesday nights this next coming year.

This brings my journey up to the present time that we are living in.

After reading the chapter "Rebuilding My Life," the pieces start to fall into place, just like putting a jigsaw puzzle together one piece at a time, and soon we will be able to see the whole picture.

CONFIRMATIONS

Behold, I stand at the door and knock.
If anyone hears My voice and opens
the door, I will come in to him and dine
with him, and he with Me. To him who
overcomes I will grant to sit with Me
on My throne, as I also overcame and
sat down with My Father on His throne.

Revelation 3:20-21

One day in 2004, when W. D. was at my house, I received a telephone call from Brian, and his letter came in
the mail. I said, "W. D., you must read this letter!" The letter
went on to say that in 2003, Brian was in a bad car accident;
apparently, he died, and God brought him back to life. He
was at Jeannette Hospital in the ICU when this occurred.
Brian was telling me all about his experience and that God
was talking to him about his life and what he must do. What
God told him that he was to make amends with everyone he
had hurt right before his eyes. Brian thought I was his soul
mate; he could see me besides God. Brian said, "Of all the
people in my life, I saw you with God." I don't believe Brian
hurt me. It was his ex-wife that he truly hurt and needed to
make amends with her. I believe after meeting Dawn, the

message from God that I received, she was his soulmate, and he truly hurt her. Dawn told me she was with Brian the day of the accident. Then she was at the hospital, sitting by his bedside and holding his hand. As you can see from chapter one, this was the person God showed me that was dead with machines and tubes hooked up to him, and I said, "This man was dead." God said, "Not for long." This took place in 1981.

Donna,

I really cannot believe I finally got in touch with you. I have to tell you the complete truth about why I needed to talk to you and to find you. It all started on March 17, 2003, when I woke up in Jeannette Hospital after a very near-death experience. I had a visit from the lord in a very strange way; the entire vision was of you and me.

I'm not going to get into a lot of details about the accident, but I will tell you that it was the worst I have ever encountered, and that was when I decided to get my life together and ask the Lord to forgive me. The first thing that was said in the vision was, "Make amends to those you hurt while in your addiction." I knew then that God was doing for me what I could not do for myself.

Confirmations

To get to the point of the vision is to say that I was taken in spirit to a place in my heart, and in there was you. Not my ex or anyone else, but it was you. So, you can see now why I have been trying so hard for the last two years to find you. I know this must sound crazy, but the Lord was telling me that the person that I was destined to be with was right in front of my eyes, but my eyes were shut.

I know this must be a lot to swallow right now since you just received my letter, and out of the blue, we talk for the first time in over two years, but I did need to get this out. In the steps of recovery, one step sticks with me, and it says, "Make direct amends to those you hurt." So, I guess what I am trying to say is that I really screwed up because I could have had a good life with you, and I messed it up. All I want to say is that I hope you can forgive me, and if you do, can we be friends? If anything else would come from that, then, I guess, I could say that the Lord is definitely with me.

Thank you for letting me get this out, and if you still want to talk and be friends, I will always be here...

God bless you and thank you,

Brian Defelice

Amen, Amen, Amen

In 2008, my boss asked the question, "Who wants to work at Jeannette Hospital?" I heard God's voice say, "I want you to go." Immediately, I raised my hand, and I said, "I will go." So I went to work there. I was obedient to God's voice. In 2009, due to limited staff, I was able to work in the ICU. I was in the room; I believe Brian was in when he had his car accident. I had goosebumps, amazed and in awe; I was looking up, saying, "Wow! These are truly miracles that God has performed!" How awesome that this had happened. God is *awesome*! I was thinking how in 1981 I was beside God, looking down at Brian lying in bed in this exact room. In 2003 when Brian was looking up at God and me, now I was standing in this very same room in 2009. I worked at Jeannette Hospital for a year and a half. Then I had to go back to work at Westmoreland Hospital. Jeannette Hospital is now closed. What are the chances of that ever happening? God made this all possible. I give God all the honor and glory.

In March 2005, Christopher had to have surgery to get his tonsils removed. W. D. was there supporting Christopher and me. W. D. stayed as long as he could in my life. He toughed it out; then, one day, he could not take it anymore and walked out the door. I use to say, "If I could leave, I would." But I am too committed to my children, whom I love, and God, who I love regardless of my circumstances. I heard God's voice one day; He said, "I want you to give him up." It was very clear what I had to do. W. D. left my life at the end of the month. We talked a few times after that. One time that we talked on the telephone, the Holy Spirit worked through me to give W. D. a message about his dream was to come true and a few things he must do for this to happen. Our relationship quickly came to an end. It took me a very long time to get over W. D., but I still have wonderful memories that we created. I know that God sent him into my life. W. D. married C.D. from our church. He is very involved with the church. I can finally say I am so happy for him; he is blessed. But I cannot help to think God has a big plan for his life that he needs to fulfill yet. It is for his dream to come true. His cup could be running over with overflowing blessings for the abundant life God has promised him. God has promised this to everyone: the abundant life fulfilling God's personal plan He has planned for you by being obedient to God. God loves us and wants to bless us anyway. We all just need to receive His plan for our life. W. D. was out of my life; however, we still attend the same church; I give God all the glory and honor for this.

In February 2006, on a Tuesday, I attended the ladies' Bible class and sat at a table with a few wiser women of the church. I met two wonderful ladies E. T. and A. S. The following Tuesday, I had to go to work, so I could not attend the ladies' Bible class. The very next Tuesday, I was able to make it and sat at the same table as before with Eve and Ann. Eve said, "Donna, "I have something for you." I said okay. E. T. said, "I was shopping at Oldies, and God told me to buy this for Donna." She repeats that same saying three times. Eve went on to say, "I don't know what it means, so consider this a gift from God." E. T. put my gift in front of me; it was wrapped up in yellow tissue paper. I opened it up. I was so excited, I said, "I know what this means; God told me whenever I get to the place I want you to be, I will give you the key." It was a brass holder holding scripture cards with a fancy key on the front of the box. This is the key God mentioned that I would receive; from chapter four of this book. My friend W. D. and I discussed the same key back in September 2003 that I had faith in receiving when I did not have it yet. Thank you, Jesus; I give you all the praise, glory, and honor forever. Amen, Amen, and Amen.

During the football season of 2007, my children played for East End Steelers. I met a football mom who was a Christian and became a close friend. She held a ladies' Bible study in her home on Monday nights. I would attend; we were holding ourselves accountable for God. My faith was growing stronger in the Lord at this point in my life. I was hearing God's voice in my life, and one thing I was to accomplish for His kingdom was that God wanted me to sign up for love and seek.com, but only until my membership ran out, then I was not to sign up again. I said, "Okay, Lord, I will do it." I met a few guy friends only to email a few times; that was all. Then I heard God's voice through the Holy Spirit telling me He wants me to tell these men to seek Him first, ask Him who it is whom God wants them to be with for their special one that they are supposed to be with. I said, "How am I going to know what men to say this to?" God answered, "The men that click on your name, email them what I said." I cannot remember exactly what was said a long time ago. It went something like this: whenever two people want to meet their special someone, ask God first, they are on the same level spiritually, and God will make this all possible for them to be together. When they get together, there is a strong, powerful bond that no man can break, and their cup will be running over with blessings, and they will get so much accomplished for His kingdom. I started to send this out the hard way typing each and every time that someone clicked on my name. At first, I had one click a day; then, it started to increase more each day. I was wondering how this was going to be possible to get this message out. I was telling my oldest son about how I was typing this message out each and every time. He said, "Mom, let me show you an easy way: all you have to do is click one button, and the message will be sent." I did not have to type the message to every person every time. Boy, I was thankful for my son's input. I went to my ladies' Bible study, and as soon as it was over, I rushed home because my membership was just about to expire. I went on my site to find out I had about one hundred messages to respond to. I started to click away. I wanted to give these men their messages before the time was up at 9:00 p.m. I remember praying that I will be able to reach everyone with this message before my membership has expired. I was relieved that I made it. Just as I thought I was finished, I received another message. "*Oh, no!*" I said. "I have to send out another message." I thought I must hurry before I run out of time. I then heard God's voice say, "No, I want you to send a special message this time." This man's question was, "What does it mean for your cup to be half empty or running over?" He believed his special someone knew the answer to his question. *Wow!* I know now that I have to type a special message this time; I cannot use the same message as the other one hundred. I am amazed. I start out by saying, "I know the answer to your question, but I am not your special someone." The special message goes like this: I had an encounter with God when I was fourteen years old. I was up in heaven; God was giving me my purpose. God said, "There was someone else up here getting their purpose too." I could not see him. God said to me, "I am giving you the answer to his question, but you are not his special someone." When two people meet that are meant to be together with their special someone that God brings together, there is so much power that their bond is strong that no man can break, and you two will accomplish much more for His kingdom. Here is the answer to your question, if you get with someone that is not your special someone, your cup will always be half empty. When you meet your special someone, their cup is half full, and your cup is half full; when you two get married, then your cup is full. Then God blesses it, and it's running over with blessings. If you get together with someone else, your cup may be full but not running over with abundant blessings, and you will still be blessed. Since you know the answer to your question and I am not your special someone, now you will be able to find your special someone. I was curious to see where this man was from; I thought he was from California, and when I looked at his profile, I was right—he was from California. It was 9:00 p.m. my membership had expired. I clicked off, and I do not know whatever happened with the situations with all of those men. I do know I did my part, God will do His part, and I give God all the honor and glory. Amen, Amen, and Amen.

On September 29, 2008, my divorce was final from J. J. L., my children's father. I still was trying to have something done legally. We were still fighting a custody battle. My attorney wanted me to subpoena my friend W. D. to testify on behalf of my children's behavior. My attorney made up the papers and sent them to W. D., but they came back saying the address was wrong. We did not have enough evidence to go to trial; instead, my attorney decided to move forward with the divorce since it has been eight years already.

On Wednesday, December 10, 2008, at church, I was really in the spirit; I was hearing God's voice talking to me through the Holy Spirit. I was given instructions while I was leaving the service. I was trying to talk to my friend C. F., but I could not focus on what she was saying. I kept hearing God's voice, "I need you to leave now." I said, "I'm sorry, C. F., I just can't focus on what you're saying. I keep hearing God's voice telling me to leave, so I must leave." She said, "Okay, just go, go." So I started skipping down the hallway out the front door and down the sidewalk. All of a sudden, I was stopped dead in my tracks; W. D. put his face in my face. I did not say a word out loud to W. D. I was thinking, *What?* I immediately asked God, "What do You want me to do?" Then instantly, it was like a light pushing down to His soul; I could smell a bad odor, then it went away. I said, "That was not that bad." Then I heard God say, "Now leave." I took a few steps, then I heard, "Now stop!" I was in front of W. D. God told me to say, "This was for my kingdom and my righteousness." I did say, "This was for His kingdom and His righteousness." I heard God say, "Now leave." I started to leave then I heard, "Now stop!" I was in front of C.D.; God told me to say, "This was for my kingdom and my righteousness." I did say, "This was for His kingdom and His righteousness." Then I heard God say, "Now leave." So I did just that, I was leaving, then I turned my head over my right shoulder to look behind me. I could see W. D. with a bright light lit all around him. He had his hands lifted up, as surrendering to God, I could tell he was in God's presence. Then I heard God say, "Now stop!" I stopped. I was at the end of the sidewalk about to step down into the parking lot, but I stopped at the very end of the sidewalk. Then, I heard God's voice again say, "Okay, give a shout of victory! As loud as you can, so the top of the mountains could hear you." I yelled hallelujah! As loud as I could so the top of the mountains would hear me. Then I left praising God. I was giving God all the Glory for delivering me from this situation.

In May 2009, a woman showed up at my door; her name

was Ann. She said, "God sent me here; I am here to help; you need help." I said, "Come on in!" I was given God's praise at this moment for sending Ann to my house to help me, for I needed help. Ann was a therapist here to see K. L. for her wraparound service visit. I told Ann I believe that I mentioned my vision that I had when I was fourteen. In my vision, there was an advocate of the court, and I believe it was Ann. She told me that she was an advocate for women. By the way, the court situation has not happened yet, according to my vision. Everything happens in God's timing; for now, it's not the right time. One day, Ann came for a visit; she had gotten her hair cut; K. L., my daughter, wanted to know who cut her hair. Ann said, "Erica cut my hair." This name seemed to trigger K. L.'s behavior. She started to say, "Erica is going to get you!" Repeatedly she said, "Erica is going to get you!" Respecting my daughter's wishes, I will not tell you my daughter's story. Nicholas was already in the kitchen; he states, "Nothing ever happened!" C. L. walks into the kitchen at the same time this is going on. He states, "Oh, I made that up!" Ann said, "So, are you the one who started all of this?" C. L. and I were quiet. I was just watching and listening to everyone and how Ann was handling all of this. I was so relieved for once; I did not have to handle the situation. Ann wrote everything down that happened. She said,

Confirmations

"Give this to your attorney." Ann left when her visit was over. I believe this was the last time we saw Ann. I gave my attorney the papers from Ann. He did not have anything good to say about the papers. He responded by saying, "Your children are too old for their grandmother; you don't have anything to worry about now." We want to believe that she has stopped with my children. I cannot help but think there are other grandchildren who are not five and eight years old yet. I pray that she is truly stopped from inappropriate touching little children. My attorney made sure that we got an appointment at The Child's Place. I am not going to say what happened, but I will say this: we got a report, and the interviewer said not to bring them back ever again.

I showed one of the pastors from my church the report, and she was very helpful. Pastor Elaine summed it all up for me; she said, "They could not say it happened, nor it did not happen. They did not rule sexual abuse out." She said, "Take this to your attorney." I did just that. My attorney was not nice about it. He kept saying, "Well, the kids are too old for her now." Needless to say, it ended with that. My attorney assured me I had nothing to worry about. He did say, "The law has changed; they have up to age fifty, no longer is it up to age eighteen to file charges against their grandmother." I asked, "Will they ever file charges against their grandmother?" I just don't know the answer to that question.

In March 2010, Cindy called me up to see if I could help pass out water for the evolution team as part of the motorcycle club at our church. I said, "I would do it." I met a few nice people; then I sat down by a person, he was a very good singer. I connected with him; my dad used to sing to me when I was a child. As we were talking, I found out his name was D. P. I asked him what kind of motorcycle he had. I said, "Is it a nice bike?" He said, "Yes, why? Do you want a ride?" I said yes. Well, we started dating, and we were in a deep relationship for eleven months, then it all ended. My children used to call him D. P. the muffin man; he would bring them muffins. It seemed like D. P. brought joy to our lives again. We created a lot of memories that were fun. D. P. showed Nicholas how to shoot a gun and took him hunting. Chris got to help D. P. drag a deer. This meant so much to my boys; their dad never went hunting with them. My daughter, on the other hand, was not so pleasant to be around. She was mean at times. Well, time to move on, I realize God wants what's best for me, and I must wait longer to get God's best for my life. I pray that I will be able to receive the blessings that God has for my family. I know it is going to take being faithful to God, patients, God's timing, perseverance, righteousness, peace, love, being thankful for everything, prais-

Confirmations

ing and trusting God to bring about a fulfilled life in Jesus. I am doing my best, living for Jesus. Being obedient to God's voice, I know I'm being led down my rightful path that God has for my life.

I want to share a few scriptures with you. Matthew 19:26, "But Jesus looked at them, and said to them, 'With men this is impossible, but with God all things are possible.'" First Timothy 6:11 (KJV), "But thou, O man of God, flee these things; and follow after righteousness, godliness, faith, love, patience, meekness." First Thessalonians 1:3 (KJV), "Remembering without ceasing your work of faith, and labour of love, and patience of hope in our Lord Jesus Christ, in the sight of God and our Father." First Thessalonians 5:24, "He who calls you is faithful, who also will do it." Luke 8:15 (KJV), "But that on the good ground are they, which in an honest and good heart, having heard the word, keep it, and bring forth fruit with patience."

> Oh, love the LORD, all you His saints! For the LORD preserves the faithful, And fully repays the proud person. Be of good courage, And He shall strengthen your heart, All you who hope in the LORD.
>
> **Psalm 31:23-24**

Amen, Amen, Amen

First Corinthians 1:9 (KJV), "God is faithful, by whom ye were called unto the fellowship of his Son Jesus Christ our Lord."

> There hath no temptation taken you but such as is common to man: but God is faithful, who will not suffer you to be tempted above that ye are able; but will with the temptation also make a way to escape, that ye may be able to bear it.
>
> **1 Corinthians 10:13 (KJV)**

February 10, 2011, K. L. talked to her school therapist about what her grandmother did to her. This was the first time she talked about the situation to anybody since she talked to Ann two years before. There has not been any inappropriate behavior in a long time with the children. But on November 9, 2011, around 4:30 p.m., K. L. had inappropriate behavior. I'm not going to write about her behavior, but it was very inappropriate. Ann once said, "Every behavior has a purpose."

Since November 2011, around Thanksgiving, God has been doing new things in my life. He has put it on my heart to join the choir at our church. I heard God's voice saying, "I want you to join the choir." I made a deal with God. I said, "If this is from you, then I will have to hear that they are in need of singers then; I will join up." I was saying in my thoughts, *You know D. P., he is in the choir.* Trying to respect D. P.'s thoughts, at least what I think they would be, I said, "D. P. cannot stop me from doing things in the church for God." I said to God, "I must be sure this is from you before I do anything." This is why I wanted to hear that they were in need before I joined the choir.

On Sunday, January 15, 2012, Pastor Tom announced the choir was in need of singers. In my heart, I knew I had to do this. I called the choir director and joined the choir; that same evening, I went to choir practice. It turned out this was the first practice; I didn't miss anything. This was in God's perfect timing. I really believe I am going to enjoy the choir. I am looking forward to being a blessing in someone's life and being blessed. I am not sure what God has planned for me here, but I will find out by continuing my walk with Jesus.

Over the next couple of months, I will be moving out of my parents' house; after eight years. My friend M. C. has been a true friend over the past five years that I've known her. She has half a duplex that we can rent. I am so thankful for my friend M. C. She even taught me to ride my Honda Rebel 250. We only went on a few rides together, but we are planning more. I love to ride. I'm not sure if all of my children will be moving with me or not. Nicholas is eighteen years old; he lives with his dad to attend Mount Pleasant

School. Chris is fifteen years old; he just moved in with his dad in August 2011, also to attend Mount Pleasant School. He stays with me at times and goes to church with me. Chris is starting to get connected at the Word of Life, attending class, and getting to know new friends. I am so blessed and happy for Chris. K. L. is now thirteen years old; she will be changing schools and living with me. She will be attending church again. God's word does not come back void; I am trusting and believing God for His promises. Amen, Amen, and Amen!

In April 2014, I met my new neighbor, J. J. L. He was very nice. I needed work done around the house before Easter that week. He decided that he would help me get the work done. He was a very hard worker and accomplished much. I asked him, "Would you like to go to my church with me?" He said yes. Presently, as I'm writing this, he is still attending my church. J. J. L. became a good friend, and he is very helpful in my life. He still helps my family and me whenever we need him and vise-verse. He is a good neighbor.

This year, 2016, is definitely a year full of changes in my life. I am looking forward to this year as many positive things will happen in my life.

> And not only that, but we also glory in tribulations, knowing that tribulation

produces perseverance; and perseverance, character; and character, hope.
Now hope does not disappoint, because
the love of God has been poured out in
our hearts by the Holy Spirit who was
given to us.

Romans 5:3-5

On March 20, 2016, I received a phone call from my
new prayer partner, who I met through my friend Melanie.
His name is Roberto. He has been an encouragement and
inspiration in my life through his poems that he creates and
his prayers over my family—all of which he is guided by the
Holy Spirit to say and do.

On April 27, 2016, I received the good news that my son
Christopher got his brand new adult tooth put in by his dentist, which the Marines had paid for. This was such a wonderful blessing for Christopher. From the picture that he sent
me, it looks white and very nice. Thank you, Lord Jesus!

On April 17, 2020, I received news that Brian was back
in the hospital and on the floor that I work on. I only saw
him one other time in the hospital when we had spoken brief-
ly to one another. Well, during his stay in the hospital, we
were able to speak to each other; on this day, he actually
apologized to me for the things he put me through with his
alcoholism while we were married. There was too much to

write down and not worth remembering all of it. I told him I was sorry for whatever I may have done to him. We have forgiven each other. I am thankful we had this opportunity; you see, Brian is dying, his body has taken a toll from the alcohol for many years. His liver, kidneys, and pancreas are all damaged. God has given him a second chance of life, brought him back to life in March 2003. God wanted me to do something in his life from chapter four when I was fourteen and had an encounter with God up in his house. Here we are, living out our lives; we were only married eight months, then divorced from July 2012 to March 2013. I believed he would kill me somehow. All of the sinful things going on, like adultery, witness him kissing a girlfriend; there were many girlfriends. We then went our separate ways after explaining to him my side of the story where Brian did see me with God. I was fourteen years old, and God brought him back to life. I did all I could do to help Brian in his life; I told him to quit taking from people. I stressed how God gave him a second chance at life. He should appreciate it. To no avail, Brian did not change in his life. After many years later, here we are in a time such as this, I had the opportunity to talk to Brian again only because of my job; I work at the hospital. I am very thankful I was able to talk to him again about what God has done for him in his life. You see, the hospital is

Confirmations

not allowing any visitors in with the pandemic going on this COVID-19. I'm not sure Brian is comprehending all of this. I am still trying to help him when we talk on the telephone. I gave him a spiritual book to read, and I gave him the book that I am writing so far to read while he was in the hospital. I told Brian I wanted him to read this book; he was in it. To no avail, he has not read it yet. As of today, May 3, 2020, we had a conversation, and I asked him on the telephone. I am only on chapter three and just entering into this event that happened in my life. We were talking about how he needs a liver to survive then later a kidney. Just pray for Brian; he is still here; God has a plan for his life for good, not evil. I pray Brian will allow God to soften his heart so he can hear God's voice in his life and be led by the Holy Spirit to instruct him right from wrong, so he will be able to make better choices in his life. Brian was the friend that brought me to the Word of Life, my church from chapter four. God said, "I will lead you to a place that doesn't exist through a friend, but it will." In 1981, the Word of Life didn't exist. This was when I was fourteen years old and was up in heaven in God's house. God truly exists today.

After this chapter of my life, I had joy and peace in my life like never before, and words just can't describe the amazing sense of stillness, which brings me to my next chapter "Peaceful Minds."

PEACEFUL MINDS

Peace came after the storms in my life. The big storm was the evilness my mother-in-law has done to her son, my children, and a few other people. By her behavior, their lives were all shattered. The other storms in my life were the split-up of my marriage, custody battles, my children's behaviors, and our relationships before and after these storms.

> Do not think I came to bring peace on earth. I did not come to bring peace but a sword. For I have come to "set a man against his father, a daughter against her mother, and a daughter-in-law against her mother-in-law"; and "a man's enemies will be those of his own household." He who loves his father or mother more than Me is not worthy of Me. And he who loves son or daughter more than Me is not worthy of Me. And he who does not take his cross and follow after Me is not worthy of Me. He who finds his life will lose it, and he who loses his life for My sake will find it.

Matthew 10:34-39

Finally, all of you be of one mind, having compassion for one another; love as brothers, be tenderhearted, be courteous; not returning evil for evil or reviling for reviling, but on the contrary blessing, knowing that you were called to this, that you may inherit a blessing. For "He who would love life And see good days, Let him refrain his tongue from evil, And his lips from speaking deceit. Let him turn away from evil and to good; Let him seek peace and pursue it. For the eyes of the LORD are on the righteous, And His ears are open to their prayers; But the face of the LORD is against those who do evil."

1 Peter 3:8-12

John 14:27, "Peace I leave with you, My peace I give to you; not as the world gives do I give to you. Let not your heart be troubled, neither let it be afraid."

MY FIRST MARRIAGE GETTING PEACE

I thought I had the perfect marriage. I was married for eight years, and I was living my dream. We attended the Church of Christ in Connellsville, Pennsylvania, every Sunday morning and Wednesday night services as a family, and that was all I ever wanted in my life for my whole family to go to church together and hear God's word. Also, I was a stay-at-home mom and did not have to work. I had so much peace in my life. Then one day, the storm came and hit hard. A family secret that was kept a secret for many years—affected my children and me. God was using me to shout this secret from the mountain tops, and, as you can see, it's no longer a secret. My marriage was destroyed by the evilness of my mother-in-law's behaviors. Getting divorced meant custody battles that were very ugly, the children traveling back and forth between our houses. After my husband (now ex-husband) told his side of the story of his family secret to me, then he turned on his own family, us, and took his parents' side, and denied the whole thing. At this time, I was dealing with his family secret, the split of my marriage, my children's bad behaviors, the games of my in-laws trying to turn my children against me, and my husband (now ex-husband) choosing the evilness from his own mother's bad behaviors. I was devastated! The questions would go through my mind; *How could this be happening to me, to us? How can I repair the damage that was done to my children?* My oldest son had to be sent away to get therapy, or the state was going to put him in foster care, and I would not be able to see him again. It was at home to receive therapy 24/7 around the clock by living with the therapist. My relationship with my son was broken at such a young age.

In summary, the evilness that had entered my family from my father-in-law and mother-in-law, the destruction of breaking up a marriage, and causing trauma to the children from their inappropriate behaviors. The children were acting out and needed therapy. We spent many hours in appointments so they could get their therapy. We were forced to move out of our little house the stability broken that my children knew. I had to go back to work whenever I was a stay-at-home mom for eight years. My children only knew me to be at home with them. Many changes were made. We had many court dates for child support. My life was turned upside down. My mother-in-law would scream in my face in public whenever she would see me. I had to file harassment charges against her. We were all ordered into therapy. My mother-in-law became so angry in our sessions that they canceled her therapy. I continued with the therapy sessions along with my children until the therapists thought we were all fine and didn't need therapy anymore. I used to say that I had so much therapy that I could be a therapist. After all that I had been through with therapy sessions, I truthfully don't want to be a therapist. My church family would try to help me through all of this, which I am forever grateful to have so many sisters in Christ who truly cared for me. One of my dear sisters in Christ, Janet, would tell me this was a generational curse that needed to be broken and stopped with my children so it would not be passed down to their children. That is what I did with my children, breaking this curse that it will not go on anymore in Jesus' name, Amen! She has passed away since I started writing this book. I will always remember her for how she has helped me. I had a dear sister in Christ who was my mentor; she would write me letters caring and loving on me just as God would want her to. God has brought so many people in and out of my life over the years, and they're all my family. I love God, knowing He loves and cares for me. God loves and cares for you too. The years have gone by as the children grew up, and all of this is in the past, but justice is in the future. My family did not get justice. We got much peace through God's way. God's will be done, not my will, in this situation.

After the storms in my life, we were redefining relationships, as the therapist would put it. I spent the next several years repairing my oldest son's and my relationship that was broken. This was not an easy task; we had many obstacles to climb through, many doctors' appointments, therapy sessions, and therapists coming to my home. The peace I received the most was from the therapist Ann. The first time

Amen, Amen, Amen

Ann knocked on my door, I opened it up—she was standing there and said, "God has sent me here." I replied, "Well, come on in then!" I was beside myself and needed answers. I had joy whenever Ann came to my house. She was the therapist for my daughter, K. L., with her knowledge, gifts from God, she was able to get the truth to come out; my daughter talked about her situation with her grandmother's evil behaviors, my sons talked about it what they remembered. I had this sense of relief that the children finally talked that this was all true what their dad said about his mother and their family secret that was no longer a secret! Hallelujah, praise God for revealing the truth. Thank you, *Lord*, in Jesus' name, Amen, Amen, and Amen!

This was not a lie but the truth. All the time, they called me crazy and a liar; you see who lied now. For the truth to come out was a sense of freedom for me to be able to move forward in my life. The second time I felt this freedom was when, the district attorney, asked me to come to the office to take a lie detector test; I did not hesitate, and I said yes! Once I had arrived, I found out that J. J. L., my ex-husband, his father, and his mother all refused to take the lie detector test. I can't say that I was surprised to hear they were not taking the lie detector test that just goes to show you they were covering up the truth about what happened to my children and trying to protect the family's secret by betraying their own grandchildren. I wasn't surprised that J. J. L. was in denial, still choosing his parents' side of the story. I went into the office, and a person gave me the test. I was nervous the first time taking a lie detector test. It was over, and the results were in to hear that I was not lying. I was telling the truth, and it was proof for me and the courts. The district attorney said, "You don't have anything to worry about— you are telling the truth." This came about after my daughter talked after the courts already knew the story her brothers told, and I was trying to protect my daughter from her grand-mother from doing this again, but it happened to her, too, at age eight. I felt that the system failed my family. Then once I had this lie detector test, I felt so much relief and felt like some baggage dropped off of my body. I felt lighter. It was my mind relaxing and enjoying the moment of truth. I was finally happier in my life and moving forward. All the truth will come out someday; maybe get justice for the situation; I can assure you vengeance is God's.

The third time I felt this sense of relief crying tears of joy was just this summer, my son at age twenty-six, was sitting on my bed as I was writing this book back in the summer months of this year 2020, and he shared with me his side of the story and what he remembered whenever he was five years old to eight years old. I felt like the truth came out, and our mother-son bond was restored. I felt very close to my son while he was talking and opening up his feelings to me. I'm sorry he had to go through all of this in his childhood from evilness. I just wanted him to have a good life.

The fourth time I felt this sense of relief crying tears of joy was when my son did a video on YouTube. On December 23, 2020, I clicked on a video that was by Nicholas Lucia, my son. I was joyful and crying when I heard him tell of his testimony of his life when he was six years old and sexually abused by a family member. He did not give details just by him saying that was confirmation that this did happen. For all of you who didn't believe my situation, here is the confirmation that something did happen to my family. This was long overdue; Nicholas was not ready to talk about this before in his life; this took twenty-one years before he was comfortable to express the pain in his life. I consider this a breakthrough, and he can move forward in his life. I am so happy for my son to be able to put all of this behind him and move forward in his life. He can become successful in whatever he decides to do in his life.

Whenever the children were small, I decided to date after my first divorce. I found some peace in that I was able to move forward in my life. I met Brian, W. D., and D. P. I met

W. D.; he wanted to get married—I just wasn't ready with everything I have gone through. So everything ended, and W. D. married a woman from our church. For some reason or another, it was a hard situation: I kept going to church and watching them; we all went to the same church. One day after church, W. D. put his face in mine; I had no idea what that was about; I immediately went to God and said, "*Lord, what do you want me to do?*" Immediately the *Lord* spoke, "Say this is for my kingdom and righteousness, take a step to my left and stop; say this is for my kingdom and righteousness, then leave, then stop, and give a shout of victory!" I did all the Lord instructed me to do; I said that in front of W. D., then I step to my left, I said that in front of C.D., and then I left; I looked over my shoulder, and W. D. had light all around him, and his hands were lifted up praising God, and I stopped, I was at the end of the sidewalk, then I gave a loud shout of Hallelujah with my right arm raised up in the air. Then I proceeded to the parking lot to find my car, so I could leave the church. That was so powerful; I had so much peace in my life over that situation. I definitely got my victory over that situation. Then D. P. I was grateful to of met. He took Nicholas hunting, something I could not do as a single mom. We rode our motorcycles together, which was nice to gain a friend. That when I was thinking outside my box and learned to ride a motorcycle. D. P. decided to marry someone his own age; he was much older than me. I received so much peace from that situation.

> Be anxious for nothing, but in every-
> thing by prayer and supplication, with
> thanksgiving, let your requests be made
> known to God; and the peace of God,
> which surpasses all understanding, will
> guard your hearts and minds through
> Christ Jesus.
>
> **Philippians 4:6-7**

Time has gone by so quickly, and now that my children have become adults, this battle is their battle; I did every-thing I thought I needed to do as a parent. I tried to have something done about this, to no avail; this is how it all came about with no justice from the court system.

All of our battles belong to the Lord whenever we cast all of our care upon Him. The Lord always sees us through to the other side.

MY SECOND MARRIAGE GETTING PEACE

Whenever I first met Brian, he was a true friend. The first thing and the best thing he ever did for me was to take me to the Word of Life Church in Greensburg, which is presently

Peaceful Minds

the church that I attend. Brian did not stay long; he left the church. Also, he would pick up my son Christopher from half a day kindergarten from school. I didn't have a vehicle at this time. I enjoyed the peace in my life when Brian was a big helper to me. Brian started drinking again, left the church, and ran off to get married. I lost contact with him for many years. I was getting back on my feet and moving forward in my life. As you can see, God told me He would lead me to a place that didn't exist but will through a friend. This happened to my friends; Brian took me to the Word of Life church. He was my friend; the church didn't exist whenever I had my encounter with God at the age of fourteen. This is powerful confirmation.

Then in May 2012, I found Brian again; we were married by June 22, 2012. This time things didn't go so well. Brian was an alcoholic; his life was going down, he was doing everything imaginable that came along with alcohol. Harming his body by drinking hard liquor, women, and not caring about anyone but himself, getting in trouble with the law pulling me in by trying to get me arrested; however, he lied and got me in trouble with the law. He charged all my credit cards to the max and told me he would pay me back monthly payments. Well, he made a payment on each card then stopped making the payments. This one day, he was driving drunk with me in his truck; he was speeding, hitting potholes and bumps in the road. My head would hit the roof of his truck. I pleaded with him to stop the truck, and I would walk. He would not listen to me. However, he did say, "You're lucky I love you, or I would toss you out of this truck while it was moving." I was praying and thanking God he did not do that, and we got home safe. It could have been a lot worse. I would pray to God, asking Him what He wants me to do in his life so I could get out of this situation. I thought maybe he would try to kill me next time. Then one day, Brian said, "I know I saw you with God after my accident." This was in March 2003, and I was with God on February 4, 1981, whenever God showed me a dead man, this was Brian in the future, and I was fourteen at this time. The future was 2003. God wanted me to do something in his life, maybe to confirm he saw me with God. I'm not sure if that is what it was or just many things that had happened in our life together. After Brian and I talked in 2012 about seeing me with God after his accident in 2003, he wanted a divorce. After eight months, we were divorced. I had so much peace and relief that this was awesome, amazing how God let me see Brian as a man, and God showed Brian me as an outline, and he knew it was me. This is so powerful. Who has a story like this one?

Peaceful Minds

I haven't seen Brian in many years after the damage he caused in my life in 2012. This one day at work in January 2020, Brian was holding the elevator door open for my co-worker and me while we were getting our linen cart off the elevator. We made small talk then left. In February 2020, I was sick from a patient who coughed in my face and out of work until April 2020. I was trying to get peace while I was sick. I know my faith has grown since everything I have been through. Once, I went back to work to find out Brian has been a patient on my floor. He told me he stopped drinking seven months prior to coming to the hospital. We made peace with one another and forgave each other for everything bad that has happened in our life together. It turns out Brian was very sick and needed a liver transplant from all that drinking. Later on—many hospital stays; later to find out he was not a candidate for a liver transplant and will probably die without it. Brian and I became close friends at the hospital; I would talk, walk around outside of the hospital with him, talking about the good parts of our life together. I would bring him some chocolate milk and whatever he needed. I even cooked for him a few times. Then one day, that all changed: Brian passed away on July 16, 2020. I had peace knowing we forgave each other and became friends before he passed away. I miss his laugh.

Amen, Amen, Amen

The details are written in the previous chapters about Brian and me, the journeying we were on together, and also the letter he has written to me is in chapter eight.

While I was going through these storms in my life, whether it was small or big, I would always love the person, hate the sin, and always forgave them right away. Trusting God with my problems, together we were moving mountains and casting them in the sea. The peace of knowing God loves me and my family doesn't matter what situation arose, as long as I was seeking God first in my life and keeping my eyes fixed on *Him*. It was by God's grace that we made it through the storms.

After these storms, I did get peace in my life, but justice was not served to my family. God promised me; He showed a court seen in my life that we get justice for my children and their situation. This was the hope that I cling to during my storms; I focused on God's words to me, and my faith has grown. I will write more about this court seen in the next chapter also in my next book that will come out after we go to court to get justice for my now adult children. This will be my victory about my ex-mother-in-law's secret, or so she thought it would remain a secret, and what little did she know God had other plans for our lives.

This is a difficult time we are living in, and through all

this chaos, I have true peace by doing my job of helping others. I must say I am more exhausted than ever before. Whenever I go outside after working hard, I look up and see how amazing life truly is. I see stars shining bright, the moon shining, and it puts a smile on my face instead of wanting to cry for everyone going through this difficult time. Instead, I thank God for His creation. I have peace in knowing I'm doing the best that I can, and with Jesus, I'm able to do more. Just to mention, my book is finally getting close to the end of being created. God wanted me to write my book, through the Holy Spirit, just as I'm writing it, and not to mention the same applies as my journey continues; the Holy Spirit guides me down my rightful path *God* had planned for me right into the next chapter of my life.

THE JOURNEY CONTINUES

Joel 2:28, "And it shall come to pass afterward That I will pour out My Spirit on all flesh; Your sons and your daughters shall prophesy, Your old men shall dream dreams, Your young men shall see visions."

Just one minute, please, I would like to take this time to recap my journey thus far in my life before going into the next chapter of my life's journey. My life has not been boring, that is for sure. God has done so much, more than I could ever imagine in my life.

In summary, being a part of the B. family's life or the B. family being a part of my life, this is just how we become part of a family in Jesus Christ. I may not be a preacher's daughter or a preacher's wife, but I am a child of God, God's daughter, and I'm born into a family whenever I accepted Jesus as my Lord and Savior, and I was buried with Him in baptism. Jesus took me up to heaven in an elevator and showed me different levels on the way up to meet God in *His* home.

As I was in heaven, God showed me my life, and He gave me a task. The task was to share with this person from California; I said, "How can I do this?" I was just fourteen years old at that time, and I felt that I might need to travel or call this person over the telephone. Then I realized how I could do this if I don't have his address or telephone number. When this unfolded in my life, it was on the computer, a website, that I was able to give this person from California this message, the answer to his question, and I was not that special person he was supposed to be with. Therefore, he will be able to find his special someone just the way God had set it up to happen, and as you can see at the time, I was fourteen, there were no computers; that is why I had those exact questions that I had. I find this so amazing, incredible, and awesome how God organized *His* plan.

God showed me my purpose in life. I was to stop two evil people in this world. I wanted to know how I was going to accomplish that. It was actually two different people's evil behaviors in my two marriages. This is just what we read in the previous chapters of my book.

Whenever God showed me my life, *He* said, "You see, your life is like a puzzle; when a part of your life is fulfilled, it's like adding another piece to the puzzle, and soon once it all shall pass away, then you will see the whole picture—the puzzle will be completed."

In summary, I am blessed to have all of them who inspired me over the years of my life. I'm sure they all had a part in some shape or form to help mold me into becoming the person that I am today, a woman of great faith. I thank God for bringing such amazing people over the course of my life to help me get through my trials, show me what great faith is, and simply love one another; therefore, I am very grateful—especially going through a divorce; who I had planned to be married to for the rest of my life. My world had shattered, and I was broken inside of me. I was asking the question, *Why divorce?* I knew God did not like it, but God was speaking, "I have a better life for you than that." That is what God was showing me with my special gift—the key with the scripture cards. Good news, my friends, what God has done for me, He will do for you also. God loves us all.

In summary, words cannot describe the journey I had with Brian. Here is the upside of it. Brian and I shared this journey. The beginning when I met Brian in 2001 was amazing; he helped me get through my trials after my separation from my first marriage, which I am forever grateful for. Our time was short, about two months. He drove me to my church, which I currently attend at this present time. I have met some amazing families, and I met my family there. Brian was so much in love with Jesus that he inspired me in my life. I remember Brian saying to me, "Make sure you keep coming here because I'm leaving this church." He left and got married. I knew once Brian said that to me; it was definitely coming from the Lord. I was to stay at the Word of Life, so that's what I did. I knew God led me here, and I would be here until he leads me out of here. God told me I am here for the truth and to learn, and He didn't agree with everything here, but it was the best *He* had for me. After everything comes to pass from the things God showed me to live out in my life, whenever I was fourteen, *He* would lead me out of that church. God promised me then He will send me the one He wants me to be with. The only thing I remember about this is someone I already met and know. Then came this important letter. Brian tracked me down in my life to be sure I received this very important letter. His accident was on March 17, 2003, that was the day God brought Brian back to life and when he saw me with God. Do you see why this was so important to Brian? Well, he did see me with God whenever I was fourteen, and I had the most amazing encounter with God. God showed me Brian with tubes coming from his body, and I said, "This man is dead!" God said, "Not for long; I want you to blah, blah in his life." I had no idea what I was to do, but once I lived it out in my life, it was many things. I wanted to let you know I was fourteen, seeing him as a man. So this took place in 1981. In summary, the evilness that had entered my family from my father-in-law and mother-in-law, the destruction of breaking up a marriage, and causing trauma to the children from their inappropriate behaviors. The children were acting out and needed therapy. We spent many hours in appointments so they could get their therapy. We had to move out of our little house therefore the stability broken that my children once knew. I had to go back to work whenever I was a stay-at-home mom for eight years. My children only knew me to be at home with them. Many changes were made. We had many court dates for child support. My life was turned upside down. Then God showed me Brian on that day, March 17, 2003. Then on that day of his accident, God showed me to Brian—that I was with God.

Then many years later, while I was working at Jeannette Hospital, I would work in ICU but mostly telemetry. After two years of working there, the hospital made other plans for the place; as people started to leave, I stayed until the end. This one day, I went into a room, and something began to happen. I got these goosebumps. I look up to the ceiling and remember that Brian was here whenever he had his accident in 2003. He saw me with God looking down at him from heaven, and Brian was looking up at me from this hospital bed in the ICU at Jeannette hospital. That was so amazing to realize that is what had happened. Then after the employees went back over to Westmoreland Hospital to work, they closed down Jeannette Hospital. Brian's friend at the hospital gave my phone number to him so he could call me. He called, and we talked, then we ended up getting married. Our marriage only lasted eight months; then, we divorced. Brian was the opposite of how he used to be. Then I haven't talked to him in years. Then one day there Brian was at the hospital holding the elevator door open for me; he told me about his near-death experience on September 14, 2019. We didn't talk for too long. I had to get back to work. Then I got sick and missed work for about two months. When I went back to work, Brian was on my floor as a patient. This was the first time I saw him on my floor. Since then, I have seen Brian many times at the hospital. We became friends; I walked with him and brought him food. Once his appetite decreased, he would request chocolate milk. On his last request, I brought him chocolate milk and Oreo cookies. Brian and I would walk around the outside of the hospital, make small talk, and talk about good memories that we shared. Once he became too weak to walk, I pushed him in a wheelchair just a short distance only a few times. I read his letter he wrote me a long time ago, and he apologized to me for all the hurt he caused me whenever we were married. I gave him a copy of this book that I am writing now with him in it. God gave Brian a few miracles in his life. Then we had our last talk on my cell phone. Brian was getting worse. Then in the last text, he was going to talk later with me, but that never happened. I then received a text from his sister he was going. I wanted to be there, but I was at work before I could comprehend it all; he had passed away from this earth. Then the ending was amazing in gaining a friend after everything we had been through. Over a nineteen-year period, we had only been together a little over one year. The supernatural of his important letter that he wrote me was the most amazing part, and being his friend too. The end of this letter says that if we became friends, then he knew the Lord was with him. The Lord was with him. It's better to go through life with a friend and experience Jesus through them than any pleasure this earth has to offer. Life is too short to live it any other way. This one day, while Brian was a patient in the hospital, I asked him what he saw me as when he saw me with God. He replied, "I saw an outline and knew it was you." You see, Brian was one year younger than me. Life will be different at the hospital where I continue to work without Brian as a patient. My journey continues on through this life down the rightful path that God has purposed for me from the beginning of time in my mother's womb until the return of Jesus and to have eternal life with *Him*.

What have I learned through my situations? How to love

one another, forgive, have more patients, things that don't get done in one day, pour my heart out to others who may be going through the same thing to help them the best that I can do, and with God's strength, I can accomplish much. I learned that true joy is—having Christ in your life, choosing Him in all your situations, trusting and obeying Him. Prayer is powerful! The first thing to do is seek his kingdom, and all these things will be added unto you. God is faithful. What *He* says *He* will do, *He* will do it. Love your neighbor that can be anyone that God puts in your life. If anyone needs my help and I can help, I will do my very best that I can to help them. Pray for everyone that I can pray for. I have so much more peace in my life now than I had before all of this situation happened. I give God all the praise, honor, and glory; Amen, Amen, and Amen!

God showed me a court seen in my vision, but this has not happened yet. I asked God, "What do you want me to do?" God answered, "Nothing, just answer the questions." It was a courtroom session talking about my first marriage and what happened to my children. There will be justice for my family in the future. This will be book number two on what happens and my life living it more abundantly. Maybe the title of my next book will be "New Beginnings and My abundant Life."

The Journey Continues

The Lord said to me through the Holy Spirit once you live out everything that I showed you in your life, your vision will come to pass; once this happens, then your reward will be you and your special someone, the one you are supposed to be with, you will be together accomplishing much for *His* kingdom.

Whenever you have Jesus living in you, you will have everything! Give praise to the Lord; *He is King of Kings and Lord of Lords*, for *His* kingdom and for *His* righteousness! Jesus reigns *on the throne of God* in heaven to the right hand of *God*. Holy, holy, holy, Amen, Amen, and Amen!

BIBLIOGRAPHY

The Holy Bible: KJV (Copyright 1972 by Thomas Nelson Inc., Camden, New Jersey 08103); NKJV (NKJV Large Print Size Reference Bible copyright 2013 by Holman Bible Publishers, Nashville, Tennessee 37234. All Rights Reserved. The Holy Bible, New King James Version copyright 1982 by Thomas Nelson, Inc. The interior of the NKJV Large Print Personal Size Reference Bible was designed and typeset by 2KDenmark, Hojbjerg, Denmark. Proofreading was provided by Peachtree Editorial Services, Peachtree City, Georgia.)

Bevere, Lisa. *Lioness Arising: Wake Up and Change Your World. Colorado Springs: WaterBrook Press,* 2010.

Silva, Katelyn. *Idea To Print: The Step-By-Step Guide to Kick Writers Block's Butt and Finally Finish and Publish Your Book.* Self published, founder of The Author Mentor.

Myers, J. *Faith and Fear.* CD-ROM.